Ancient Egypt

Pat Waters

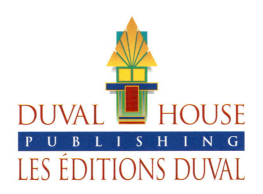

DUVAL HOUSE
PUBLISHING
LES ÉDITIONS DUVAL

S0-FQO-992

Copyright © 2004 Duval House Publishing

All rights reserved. No part of this work covered by the copyrights hereon may be reproduced or used in any form or by any means—graphic, electronic, electrostatic, or mechanical—without the prior written permission of the publisher, or in case of photocopying or other reprographic copying, a licence from Access Copyright (The Canadian Copyright Licensing Agency) 1 Yonge Street, Suite 1900, Toronto, Ontario M5E 1E5, Fax (416) 868-1261. This applies to classroom usage as well.

5 4 3 2 1
Printed and bound in Canada

Duval House Publishing

18228 – 102 Avenue
Edmonton, Alberta T5S 1S7
Ph: (780) 488-1390
Tollfree: 1-800-267-6187
Fax: (780) 482-7213
Website: http://www.duvalhouse.com

Author

Pat Waters

National Library of Canada Cataloguing in Publication

Waters, Pat

    Ancient Egypt / Pat Waters.

Includes index.
ISBN 1-55220-590-8

    1. Egypt--Civilization--Textbooks. 2. Egypt--Antiquities--Textbooks. I. Title.
DT61.W37 2004   932   C2004-900922-2

Manufacturers

Screaming Colour Inc., Friesens

Validators

Educational
Olinda Brienza, Teacher (Retired)
Waterloo Region Catholic District
    School Board
Kitchener, Ontario

Marian Reich, Teacher
Muirhead Elementary School
Toronto District School Board
Toronto, Ontario

Historical
Dr. Richard C. Smith, Professor Emeritus
Department of History and Classics
University of Alberta
Edmonton, Alberta

Bias Reviewer
Ken Ramphal, Teacher
Toronto District School Board
Toronto, Ontario

Photographic Models

Brian Daniels   Jessica Kruhlak
Warren Ip   Salina Ladha

Many website addresses have been identified in this textbook. These are provided as suggestions and are not intended to be a complete resource list. Duval House Publishing does not guarantee that these websites will not change or will continue to exist. Duval House does not endorse the content of the website nor any websites linked to the site. You should consult with your teacher whenever using Internet resources.

We acknowledge the financial support of the Government of Canada through the Book Publishing Industry Development Program (BPIDP) for our publishing activities.

Ancient Greece
The Greeks were great thinkers who are said to have invented democracy. They created remarkable works of art and architecture.

Mesopotamia
The people in Mesopotamia built the first cities, used the wheel, the plough, a system of arithmetic, and an annual calendar.

Ancient China
The ancient Chinese are known for their inventions, such as an early earthquake detector, the magnetic compass, and paper.

Ancient India
The people of the Indus Valley built carefully laid-out cities with roads and sewers, and grew cotton to make fabric.

Axum (Ethiopia)
Axum was a wealthy trading culture in Africa. Kings built tall monuments covered with writing and images above their burial chambers.

Ancient Egypt
The ancient Egyptians learned how to control the flood waters of the Nile River to irrigate their crops in the dry season.

Europe
ALPS
ROME
Mediterranean Sea
GREECE
Aegean Sea
EGYPT
Africa
Red Sea
Nile
AXUM
ETHIOPIAN HIGHLANDS
Tigris
Euphrates
Persian Gulf
MESOPOTAMIA
Asia
Indus
INDUS
HIMALAYAS
Huang He (Yellow)
Chang Jiang (Yangtse)
CHINA
Pacific Ocean
Indian Ocean
Australia

Acknowledgements

The author wishes to express gratitude to all of the people who contributed to the creation of *Ancient Egypt*. My special thanks to Karen Iversen for the vision, expertise, and guidance she provided me throughout this entire project. As well, Betty Gibbs, with her enthusiasm for ancient civilizations and her heartfelt encouragement, motivated and inspired me during this endeavour.

Thanks also to the many people who worked diligently to pull together all the components that resulted in *Ancient Egypt*. David Strand sought and gathered the beautiful photographs that bring the text to life. Claudia Pompei contributed her extensive talents to the design and production of the book. Don Hight and Carol Powers applied their remarkable artistic talents to creating the beautifully detailed illustrations, and Wendy Johnson provided the many wonderful maps essential for this topic.

In addition to the production team members, I wish to thank those people who provided feedback to ensure the authenticity of this text. Thanks to Dr. Richard Smith for validating the historical accuracy of the book's content and to Olinda Brienza, Marian Reich, and Ken Ramphal for providing their insights regarding its educational validity.

Finally, but most importantly, I extend my sincere thanks to my family. They have been patient and supportive throughout the whole process. In particular, I thank my husband, Ron Waters, who has always been there when I've needed information, discussion, or encouragement.

Project Team

Project Manager: Karen Iversen
Editors: Lynn Hamilton, Betty Gibbs, Shauna Babiuk
Cover and Text Design: Claudia Pompei, Leslie Stewart
Photo Research: David Strand
Production: Claudia Pompei, Leslie Stewart, Jeff Miles
Maps: Johnson Cartographics Inc., Wendy Johnson
Illustrations: Carol Powers, Don Hight
Photographer: New Visions Photography, Brad Callihoo
Photo Shoot Coordinator: Roberta Wildgoose

Picture Credits

Every effort has been made to identify and credit all sources. The publisher would appreciate notification of any omissions or errors so that they may be corrected. All images are copyright © of their respective copyright holders, as listed below. Reproduced with permission.

Legend: (t) top; (r) right; (l) left; (b) bottom; (c) centre; (m) middle

Cover: Jewellery, *Photo courtesy of Jon Bodsworth, The Egypt Archive*; Book of the Dead, © *The British Museum/ Heritage-Images.* Papyrus background on cover and throughout book: *Corbis ETX0077*

Courtesy of Klara Amon and Gabor Zsoldos **5** (t, b); **7** (tr); **9** (bl); **11** (br)
Courtesy of Steve Harrison **7** (bl); **11** (tl, bl)
Courtesy of Roel de Gama http://www.worldtravellers.net **7** (br); **52** (br); **53** (ml); **54** (l)
© *The British Museum/Heritage-Images* **15** (mr); **16** (b, bowl); **19** (b all); **21** (t, tube); **22**; **28** (all); **41**; **42** (tr); **45** (tr); **46** (br); **51** (all); **56** (tr, br); **57** (b); **59** (tr); **60**

Photos courtesy of Jon Bodsworth, The Egypt Archive **30** (all); **44** (bl); **46** (tr); **55** (ct, cb)
Science Museum, London/Heritage-Images **21** (t pots, b); **52** (bl)

Front endsheet, l (t) © Adam Woolfitt/Robert Harding (ml) © Upperhall/Robert Harding (b) © Sonia Halliday Photographs, photo by Verity Weston **Front endsheet, r** (t) Courtesy of Greek National Tourist Board (r) Science Museum/Science and Society Picture Library **5** (m) © Painet, Inc./fw2710/Erwin Nielsen **7** (tl) Photo by Zane Kroll **8** Earth Sciences and Image Analysis, NASA-Johnson Space Center. 23 Mar. 2004. "Earth from Space - Image Information." http://eol.jsc.nasa.gov/sseop/EFS/photoinfo.pl?PHOTO=STS077-710-91 **9** (t) © Lloyd Cluff/Corbis/Magma (mr) Worldwide Picture Library/Alamy (br) Copyright Nenadovic-UNESCO **10** © Painet, Inc./hi1309/Mediacolors **11** (tr) South African Institute for Aquatic Biodiversity **12** (tl) © Painet, Inc./en0149/William Everitt (tr) Corel 130024 (bl) Corel 130031 (br) Jeff Dawson **15** (bl) Reprinted by permission of Two-Can Publishing, an imprint of Creative Publishing International, Inc. **16** (b, jug) © Petrie Museum of Egyptian Archaeology, University College London UC8918 **18** with permission of The Reader's Digest Association Limited, *Everyday Life Through the Ages* © 1992 **19** (t) © Petrie Museum of Egyptian Archaeology, University College London UC14791 **20** © Petrie Museum of Egyptian Archaeology, University College London UC16555 **21** (t, minerals) David Strand (c) akg-images/Erich Lessing **25** (tl) akg-images/Erich Lessing (tr) Worldwide Picture Library/Alamy (b) Robert Harding Picture Library **27** akg-images/Erich Lessing **32** Courtesy of Heinemann Library, UK **34** (l) Illustration from SIGHTSEERS: ANCIENT EGYPT reproduced by permission of the publisher. Copyright © Kingfisher Publications Plc 1999. All rights reserved. (r) © Canadian Museum of Civilization, Royal Ontario Museum Collection, photographer Steven Darby, image no. S97-10867 **35** (t) Copyright 1997 by Fred Espenak, www.MrEclipse.com (b) Science Museum/Science and Society Picture Library **40** (b) Firuza Salukis, Ingrid Romanowski, Canada. **42** (tl) © Ken Gillham/Robert Harding (bl) akg-images/ Gerard Degeorge **44** (br) © Adam Woolfitt/Robert Harding **46** (ml) © CM Dixon/Heritage-Images (bm) The Virtual Egyptian Museum, www.virtual-egyptian-museum.org **49** (b) Photo by Zane Kroll **52** (t all) Photo by Zane Kroll **53** (br) Photo by Zane Kroll **54** (tr) © Neema Frederic/Corbis Sygma/Magma **55** (tl) Robert Harding Picture Library (tr) © CM Dixon/Heritage-Images (ml, mr) akg-images/Andrea Jemolo (br) akg-images **56** (l) © Archivo Iconografico, S.A./Corbis/ Magma **59** (tl) © Canadian Museum of Civilization, photographer Steven Darby, image no. S97-10845 **64** © Bettmann/Corbis/Magma **65** akg-images/Erich Lessing **67** Illustration from PYRAMIDS by Anne Millard reproduced by permission of the publisher. Copyright © Kingfisher Publications Plc 1996. All rights reserved. **69** (ml) © Roger Wood/Corbis/Magma (r, b) © Sandro Vannini/Corbis/Magma

This textbook, *Ancient Egypt*, is part of the *Early Civilizations* Series. The primary textbook for this series, *Early Civilizations*, focuses on ancient Greece and ancient China. In this textbook, we explore ancient Egypt.

Learning about early civilizations helps us better understand the way we live today. There is extensive archaeological evidence of the ancient Egyptian civilization. By studying ancient Egypt, we can discover aspects of the world today that have been inherited from ancient Egyptians. Some of these legacies may relate to your own ideas and customs.

Ancient Egypt is organized around A Model for Learning about Civilizations. The model is based on a study of the environment and the economic, social, and political elements of a civilization. This model is described on pages 4 and 5 of the *Early Civilizations* textbook. It is also found inside the back cover of this textbook.

The environment in which people live influences the economic, social, and political aspects of the civilization. People rely on their environment to meet their economic needs, such as the need for food, clothing, and shelter. As people gather and live together within a particular environment, they establish the social aspect of their culture, including language, education, arts, and religion. At the same time, people need a political structure that provides leadership and laws for living together.

Ancient Egypt offers many resources to help you with your learning. Inside the back cover, you will find three learning resources. There is a map of ancient Egypt and a timeline that shows when events occurred during the time you will be studying. You will also find A Model for Learning about Civilizations. Beside this learning model is an icon of an Egyptian merchant ship. The ship appears in each chapter to remind you of the learning model and help you identify the part of the civilization you are studying.

Photos, illustrations, maps, organizers, stories, and text information can help you better understand ancient Egypt. You will find a pronunciation guide, a glossary, and an index on the back pages of this textbook.

Throughout the textbook, you are invited to participate in activities and learn new skills. Have fun on your journey through ancient Egypt!

CONTENTS

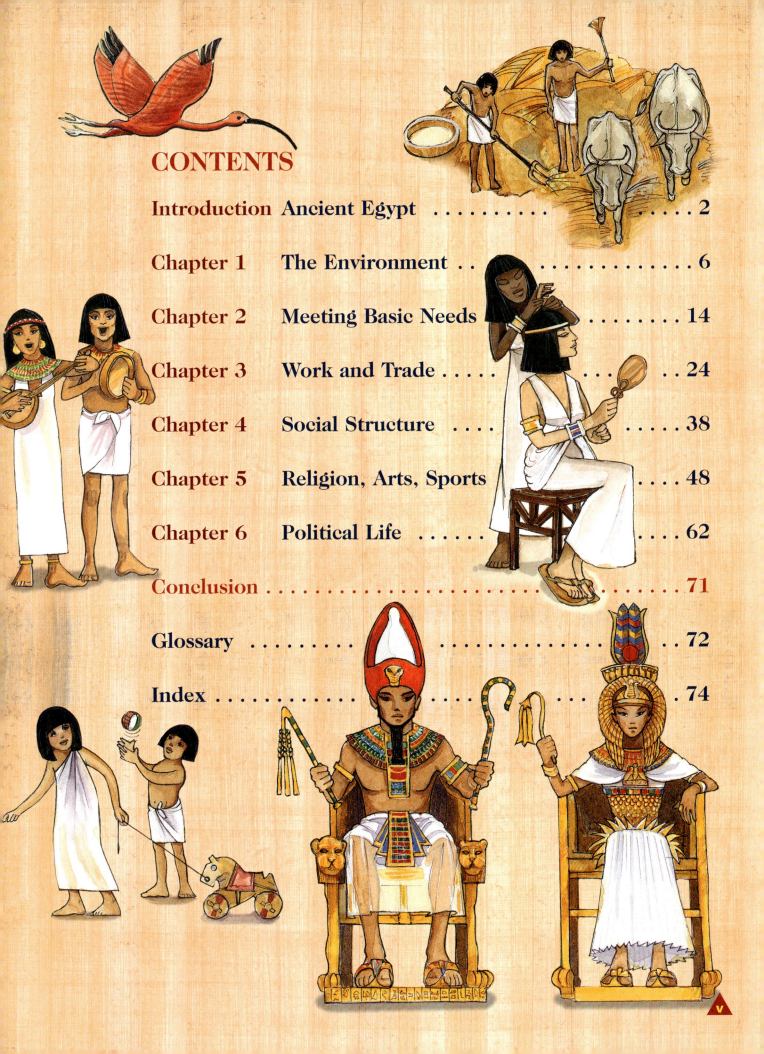

v

INTRODUCTION
ANCIENT EGYPT

The kingdom of ancient Egypt began over 5000 years ago. This civilization developed in the area where modern Egypt is today. Ancient Egyptians settled mainly along the Nile River, which was key to their survival.

The people of ancient Egypt built huge stone structures for their monarchs who were called **pharaohs**. Many of these temples, monuments, and burial structures called **tombs** have survived to the present day. Numerous artifacts have been discovered and archaeologists have learned to read the written records of ancient Egyptians, done in a form of picture writing. The archaeological remains tell us a great deal about the lives and beliefs of the ancient Egyptians.

There were many different periods in the history of ancient Egypt. This textbook will focus on the **New Kingdom**, which was the period from around 1550 BCE to 1070 BCE. By this time, the kingdom had begun to expand and incorporate many neighbouring countries. Egypt had become a powerful and wealthy country.

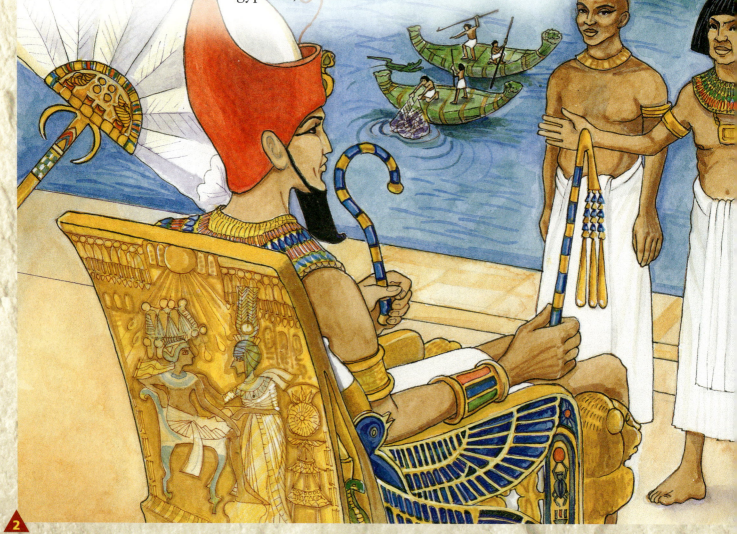

Locating Ancient Egypt

Ancient Egypt was located where modern Egypt is found today, in the northeastern part of the continent of Africa. The Mediterranean Sea formed ancient Egypt's northern border, and the Red Sea formed its eastern border.

In ancient times, Egypt covered an area of about 1 250 000 square kilometres. It was larger than the province of Ontario.

The Nile River flows from higher land in the south to lower land in the north. As a result, the northern part of Egypt was known as **Lower Egypt**, and the southern part was known as **Upper Egypt**.

Egypt was known as the country of two lands. The **Black Land** was the fertile land along the Nile that the people depended on for growing their crops. The ancient Egyptians called their homeland *kemet*, after the rich soil that was so important to them. The **Red Land** was the dry, hot, and mountainous desert land beyond the Nile River area.

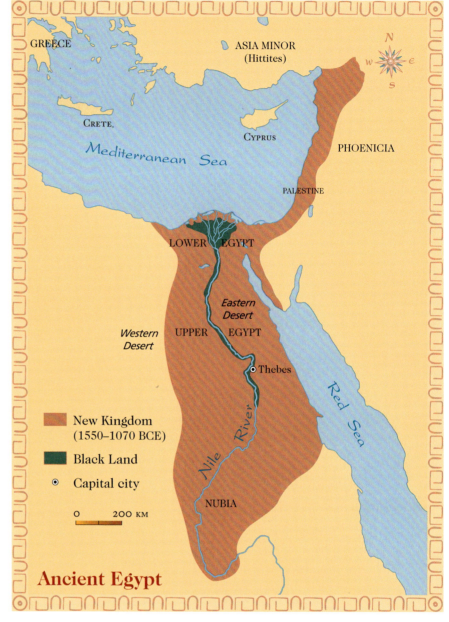

GREECE

ASIA MINOR
(Hittites)

CRETE

CYPRUS

PHOENICIA

Mediterranean Sea

PALESTINE

LOWER EGYPT

Eastern Desert

Western Desert

UPPER EGYPT

Thebes

Red Sea

Nile River

New Kingdom (1550–1070 BCE)

Black Land

Capital city

0   200 KM

NUBIA

Ancient Egypt

Do ✸ Discuss ✸ Discover

1. On an outline map of ancient Egypt, label Upper Egypt and Lower Egypt. Use colours to indicate the Black Land and the Red Land.

2. With a partner, discuss why the Nile flows from south to north instead of the other way. Write your explanation in your notebooks.

Egypt Today

The country of Egypt today is about 1 000 000 square kilometres. This is smaller than it was during the New Kingdom. It is now about the size of Ontario.

Egypt is one of the oldest civilizations in the world. It is rich in ancient art and architecture. Artifacts and archaeological remains provide a wealth of information about ancient life along the Nile River. Egypt attracts millions of tourists each year.

The city of Cairo is the capital of Egypt today.

Egypt Today

Cruise boats on the Nile take tourists to visit ancient sites.

Egyptians share their glorious past with visitors from around the world.

economic life | social life | political life

culture

the environment

Chapter 1
The Environment

Egypt is a land of many contrasts. On the banks of the Nile River, where the ancient Egyptian civilization developed, the soil is fertile and ideal for growing crops. The land beyond the Nile is made up of harsh, dry deserts, rocky hills, and high mountains. Vegetation is plentiful along the Nile and sparse in the deserts. Animals have adapted and live in each of Egypt's very different environments.

Focus on Learning

In this chapter you will learn about

- landforms and bodies of water found in ancient Egypt
- climate and vegetation of ancient Egypt
- natural resources and animal life of ancient Egypt

Vocabulary

inundation

flood plain

oasis

delta

drought

papyrus

scavenger

Landforms

Egypt has deserts where almost nothing grows. It also has some of the world's richest farmland. During ancient times, heavy rainfalls to the south caused the Nile River to flood annually. This was called **inundation**. The floods washed fine soil particles called silt onto the banks of the river, creating a flat area of land called a **flood plain**. Its top layer of soil was very fertile. Ancient Egyptians settled along the Nile because of the excellent farmland there.

Egypt's deserts are part of the Sahara, which is the largest desert in the world. The deserts do not support much life. Winds in Egypt's Western Desert constantly blow sand around, forming huge mounds called dunes.

Dunes can cover everything in their paths, even palm trees and houses.

The Eastern Desert in Egypt lies between the Nile River and the Red Sea. It has rocky hills and high mountains that are rich in oil, minerals, and stone. Some mountains on the eastern coast rise to over 2000 metres.

Egypt's deserts have oases. An **oasis** is a green piece of land that is fed by springs of underground water. Oases help plants, animals, and people survive in the desert.

To the east, the Sinai Peninsula forms a land bridge between the continents of Africa and Asia. It is mainly desert and almost completely surrounded by water. Long narrow valleys run throughout the Sinai.

Bodies of Water

The Nile River is the world's longest river. It flows 5584 kilometres from Lake Victoria in central Africa to the Mediterranean Sea in the north. The Nile follows the land as it slopes gently to the Mediterranean Sea.

The Nile **Delta** is found in the north. It is a large triangle-shaped area of land where many channels of the river empty into the Mediterranean Sea.

The Red Sea forms part of Egypt's eastern boundary. The Gulf of Aqaba lies to the east of the Sinai Peninsula and the Gulf of Suez lies to the west. Ancient Egyptians were unsuccessful in building a canal to the Gulf of Suez to link the Mediterranean Sea to other parts of Egypt.

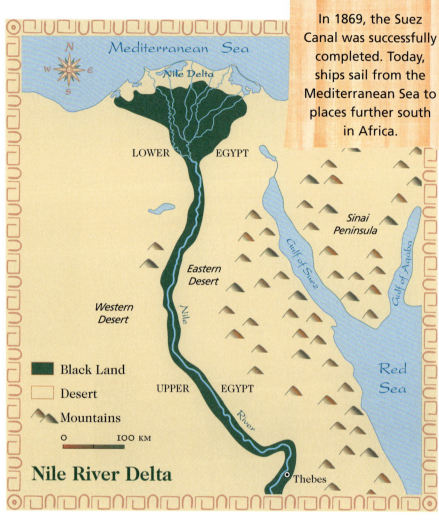

In 1869, the Suez Canal was successfully completed. Today, ships sail from the Mediterranean Sea to places further south in Africa.

Map labels: Mediterranean Sea · Nile Delta · LOWER EGYPT · Sinai Peninsula · Gulf of Suez · Gulf of Aqaba · Eastern Desert · Western Desert · Nile · Red Sea · UPPER EGYPT · River · Thebes

Black Land
Desert
Mountains
0   100 KM

Nile River Delta

These bodies of water were very important to the ancient Egyptians for food and transportation. The Egyptians especially depended on the Nile River. The fertile soil along its banks allowed them to grow healthy crops. The river was also a plentiful source of fresh water.

This photograph, taken from space, shows the most populated and fertile area of Egypt, found along the Nile River and its delta.

Do ☂ Discuss ☂ Discover

1. A river basin is the land area that drains into a river. Use a current atlas to find the names of some of the countries that are found in the basin of the Nile.

2. On an outline map, identify Egypt's main bodies of water, the Nile Delta, and how the Suez Canal links the Mediterranean Sea with other parts of Africa.

The Aswan Dams

Egyptians wanted to control the waters of the Nile so that they could be sure of a year-round supply of water. In 1902, the British completed the first Aswan Dam. In time, this dam could not fulfil all of Egypt's needs. In the 1960s, the Russians helped build another dam at Aswan called the High Dam.

The construction of the Aswan High Dam resulted in the formation of Lake Nasser.

The building of this dam threatened Abu Simbel. Abu Simbel is one of Egypt's most important historical sites. It is dedicated to one of ancient Egypt's greatest leaders. The monuments of Abu Simbel were moved to ensure their survival.

Today, Egyptians rely on the large dam. The dam allows them to store water in reservoirs (large ponds) and use it as necessary to irrigate their crops. It also provides electricity for all of Egypt.

There are thousands of kilometres of irrigation canals in Egypt.

The temples of Abu Simbel were cut apart and reassembled on higher ground to prevent them from becoming submerged in Lake Nasser.

Climate

Egypt's climate today is similar to its climate in ancient times. It is an extremely hot country with little precipitation. Its climate is affected by its location relative to the Equator. Egypt is located between 22° N latitude and 32° N latitude.

Egypt has two seasons. The winter, which is cooler, lasts from about November until April. The summer season, from about May to October, is very hot. Temperatures are highest in the southern parts of the country.

Palm trees at the Siwa Oasis were nearly stripped of all their leaves following one dust storm.

The deserts are very hot during the day, but they can be quite cool at night when the sun goes down. Sometimes, dry hot winds called *khamsins* blow the sand around at speeds up to 150 kilometres per hour. These fierce winds are so strong that they can bury objects in their paths and carry small animals around.

Egypt has very little rainfall. The areas near the Mediterranean Sea get the most rain. Further south, there is much less rainfall. Long periods of dry weather called **droughts** occur almost every summer in the south. In ancient times, heavy rainfall in central and eastern Africa flooded the Nile during the summer months. Today, flood waters are controlled with dams, and Egyptians can rely on irrigation systems during droughts.

Canada is found between 42° N and 83° N latitude.

Egyptians get almost all of their water from the Nile. An abundant supply of water and plenty of sunshine create good conditions for growing crops.

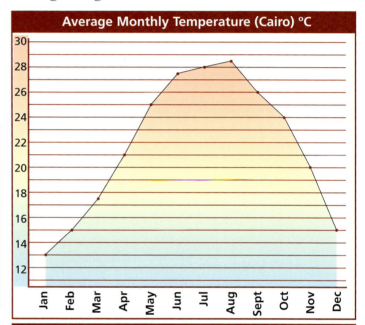

Average Monthly Temperature (Cairo) °C

Average Monthly Precipitation (Cairo) mm							
Jan	5.0	Apr	2.0	Jul	0.0	Oct	0.0
Feb	4.0	May	0.0	Aug	0.0	Nov	5.0
Mar	3.0	Jun	0.0	Sep	0.0	Dec	8.0

☥ LEGACY

The world's oldest weather records come from the Egyptians. They have been measuring and keeping records of the height of the Nile for more than 5000 years. These records provide clues about rainfall patterns and are helping scientists to better understand El Niño.

Do ☥ Discuss ☥ Discover

1. Create bar graphs to compare Egypt's annual average temperatures and amounts of precipitation to those where you live.

2. Discuss how differences in temperature and precipitation influence the way people live.

Vegetation

The natural vegetation of ancient Egypt has been somewhat changed by industrial growth and pollution. However, many plants, flowers, and grasses still grow in the marshy areas along the Nile. The lotus, which is like a water lily, grows in the channels of the Nile Delta.

The lotus was honoured by ancient Egyptians. It is seen in tomb paintings and on ancient columns.

There are few trees native to Egypt. The low amount of precipitation makes it difficult for large trees to grow naturally. Trees such as the sycamore, acacia, date palm, African fan palm, and a type of juniper grew in Egypt in ancient times.

Papyrus, a grassy reed, once grew in abundance along the Nile. It was used in a variety of ways by ancient Egyptians.

Papyrus still grows in some areas of Egypt, particularly in the south. It is used to create artwork and is also grown in decorative gardens.

Vegetation is scarce in the Western Desert. Most vegetation is found in oases. The Eastern Desert receives a small amount of rainfall. Trees such as tamarisk and acacia, along with thorny shrubs, small cacti, and aromatic herbs can grow there.

Natural Resources

In addition to its rich soil, the Nile River provided fish and waterfowl to eat. The papyrus along the banks of the Nile was used for items such as paper, baskets, and sandals. Since trees were sparse, ancient Egyptians did not have a good source of timber. However, they did use mud for making bricks.

Fish caught by ancient Egyptian fishers included carp, eel, and tilapia (shown above).

Date palms (shown above) and grapes grew in some of the oases of the desert.

For ancient Egyptians, the deserts were a source of many natural resources. Limestone and granite were quarried from the mountains of the Eastern Desert and used for building. Gold, copper, and semi-precious stones were plentiful. They were mined for jewellery and other precious objects.

Do ⚱ Discuss ⚱ Discover
1. Write a paragraph in your notebook explaining why the Nile was such an important resource for ancient Egyptians.

Animal Life

Many kinds of animals live in the water and land habitats of Egypt. In the waters of the Nile and along its fertile banks are crocodiles, hippopotamuses, and birds such as herons, ibises, and cranes. The riverbanks are also home to pintail ducks, cormorants, pelicans, and hoopoes. Frogs, lizards, and many varieties of fish such as catfish and Nile perch either live along the banks of the Nile or in the river.

Scarlet ibises live along the Nile River. Ancient Egyptians considered ibises to be sacred.

The desert is the habitat of wildcats, wild bulls, antelope, gazelles, and snakes. Hyenas and jackals also make their homes in the desert. They are **scavengers** that feed on the dead animals they find. Desert animals also hunt for prey or graze on vegetation at the edges of the flood plain. Lions and ostriches once lived in the ancient deserts, but they are no longer found in Egypt.

Ancient Egyptians hunted hippopotamuses with lassos and spears. This was dangerous because these powerful animals can be ferocious.

Ancient Egyptians hunted hyenas for meat. Hyenas are plentiful in Egypt today.

The scorpion shown here can grow to be over 10 cm in length. It is the most poisonous scorpion in the world.

In modern times, crocodile populations along the Nile River have been threatened by hunting and pollution.

Camels are often used for transportation in the desert. However, they were not regularly used in Egypt until around 525 BCE. In ancient times, Egyptians used donkeys.

Using Your Learning

Knowledge and Understanding

1. Use a chart like the one shown below to predict how the environment may have influenced the way ancient Egyptian civilization developed.

Environment	Description	Influences
Land		
Bodies of Water		
Climate		
Vegetation		
Animal Life		
Natural Resources		

EXAMPLE

2. Design a travel brochure about Egypt. Include a cover and information about vegetation, climate, animals, and landforms.

3. Begin a Vocabulary File. Write each word and its meaning on a file card. Leave room to add pictures later. File your cards in alphabetical order.

Inquiry/Research and Communication Skills

4. Read Note-making on page 21 in *Early Civilizations*. Do research on the environment of Egypt in the library or on the Internet at http://www.historyforkids.org/ learn/egypt/environment/index.htm. Make notes about new information you locate.

Application

5. Create a postcard from ancient Egypt to send to a friend. On the front, illustrate one or more of the characteristics of the environment. On the back of the card, describe how the illustration represents the environment of ancient Egypt.

6. Read Creating a Map on page 69 in *Early Civilizations*. Create symbols to represent the plants, animals, and natural resources found in ancient Egypt. Place the symbols on an outline map of ancient Egypt. Include a legend for your map.

Chapter 2
Meeting Basic Needs

The people of ancient Egypt enjoyed a successful economy because of their location. The fertile land along the Nile and the resources available to them in the surrounding deserts enabled them to meet their basic physical needs and build a magnificent civilization.

Focus on Learning

In this chapter you will learn about
- how the environment enabled the ancient Egyptians to meet their basic needs
- what foods they ate and how they obtained their food
- homes in ancient Egypt
- ancient Egyptian clothing
- health care for ancient Egyptians

Vocabulary

earthenware	ochre
mud brick	kohl
vent	henna
linen	diadem
tunic	amulet

Food

The ancient Egyptians grew crops of barley, flax, and wheat in the fertile soil along the banks of the Nile. They ground flour from wheat to make bread and cakes.

Grain was placed on a stone slab. Rubbing a stone over it changed it to a powder. Grit or husks that remained in the flour often wore down Egyptians' teeth.

Cheese was made from the milk of cows and goats. Egyptians grew vegetables such as leeks, beans, lettuce, and cucumbers. Garlic and onions were favourites.

Fruits including melons, figs, dates, and pomegranates were plentiful and important sources of food. Grapes were grown to make wine or to dry for raisins.

There was an abundance of food available. Even the poorest Egyptian people could have a healthy diet that included a variety of fruits and vegetables.

Bees were kept in cone-shaped pottery hives to produce the honey Egyptians used as a sweetener. Figs, dates, and other fruits were also used for sweetening food.

The Nile River provided fish for all Egyptians. Sometimes, they were dried in the sun or salted to preserve them for later use. Land for raising animals was scarce, and meats such as beef, pork, mutton, and goose or pigeon were too expensive for most people. Antelope, hyenas, gazelles, and waterfowl were hunted. Ostrich eggs were a treat.

This tomb painting shows a nobleman hunting birds with a throwing stick. A cat assists by frightening the waterfowl out of the papyrus marshes.

Egyptians drank wine, milk, and water. Beer was also a favourite drink. To make it, they mixed bread made from barley with water and left the mixture to ferment. The chemical change of fermenting was necessary to turn the mixture into beer.

Daily Meals

Ancient Egyptians ate two large meals a day, one in the morning and another in the evening. They dined at low tables. Sometimes, the adults sat on stools. Children sat on the floor.

Bread was a staple. In fact, it was the most important food in the ancient Egyptian diet. They made many varieties and had fifteen different words in their language for bread.

Most families ate fairly simple foods such as bread, cheese, vegetables, fruit, and fish. They drank beer or water. Wealthier Egyptians had more variety in their diets and could afford expensive meats and wines. They liked to throw lavish banquets for their friends and relatives on both solemn and happy occasions.

Most people ate off of pottery dishes called **earthenware**. The wealthy had servants who brought food to them on silver, bronze, or gold dishes. Everyone ate with their fingers and used knives made from flint. They used bowls of water to clean their fingers.

The ancient Egyptians cooked their food by roasting it over a fire on a spit (rod), grilling it on a charcoal brazier, or stewing it in clay ovens. Olive oil was used for cooking, and spices such as rosemary, cumin, garlic, parsley, cinnamon, and mustard were used to flavour food.

Meals were often cooked outside in the courtyard because it was cooler and prevented fire hazards in the home.

Red-brown clay from the Nile was used to make earthenware. Water jugs and bowls for everyday use were not usually painted or decorated.

Do ☥ Discuss ☥ Discover

1. Imagine your family lives in ancient Egypt. In your notebook, write a daily menu for your family. Sketch your family sitting at a low table for the evening meal. Label the people, foods, and beverages. Describe where and how your family would have obtained the menu items.

2. In a paragraph, describe how the environment of ancient Egypt helped provide for the people's basic need for food. Include ways that their environment limited what they ate.

A Palace on the River

Kufu and his sister Nafri leaned against the wall that surrounded the rooftop patio of their small mud brick house. They could see their mother preparing the evening meal in the courtyard below. The smoke from the brazier where she was grilling fish tickled their noses. Far down the dusty rough road, their father and his donkey were returning from the fields.

The heat of the day was stifling. As Kufu and Nafri looked out over the broad blue-green waters of the Nile, they saw large lazy crocodiles cooling themselves on the muddy riverbank. Even the birds in the papyrus thickets near the river were too hot to sing or call. A huge boat appeared far up the river, moving slowly in their direction.

When dinner was ready, the children hurried to join their parents on cushions around the low table. They were excited to talk about what they had seen. "The boat is so big and so impressive, with the sun sparkling on its white sail. Please, can we go to the river to see it?" they begged.

"All right. We will go after dinner," agreed their father. The children rushed to finish their meal of fish, bread, and beans.

When the family reached the river's edge, the majestic boat was getting closer. It had a splendidly carved masthead, a white billowing sail, and many rowers. "It's the cruise boat of a wealthy family," said their mother. "They are cruising on the river with their friends."

As the boat drew near, the children could see adults lounging on the deck and children playing board games. The men and women were dressed in brilliant white linen robes and wore glorious jewels. Elegant diadems encircled their smooth, shiny black hair, and their eyes were beautifully outlined with black kohl.

As the children stared wide-eyed, a woman smiled and waved a bejewelled hand to greet them. The children had never seen such splendour. They had never seen a palace, but this grand boat certainly must be a palace.

Later, in their low wooden beds, Kufu and Nafri talked and talked about the remarkable boat. As they drifted off to sleep, they dreamed of wearing dazzling jewels and sailing the Nile on a magnificent boat that looked like a palace.

Homes

In ancient Egypt, splendid palaces and simple huts were built of **mud bricks**. Mud was collected from the banks of the Nile and mixed with straw and stones to strengthen it. The mixture was poured into wooden frames and the bricks were allowed to dry in the sun. After the home was built, the outside walls were coated with mud plaster and painted white.

Narrow doors and small windows placed high on the thick walls provided protection from the hot sun. Shutters or mats covered the windows to keep out flies and dust. Many homes had small openings in the roof that allowed the air to circulate. These **vents** helped keep the house cool.

The walls inside the home were painted with designs or scenes from nature. Floors were hard-packed earth. Some homes had cellars for storage.

The Egyptians used the roof as an extra room. Homes were built with steps leading to the roof. There, the family could gather in the evening for a meal or to enjoy the cool breezes. Most people obtained water for their daily needs from wells.

Some of the elaborate ancient Egyptian buildings and temples had plumbing systems using copper pipes.

The front of the home was built directly on the street. Behind the home there was often a small garden. The Egyptians planted their gardens with trees for shade and fruit to eat, as well as with flowers such as daisies, cornflowers, roses, or irises.

☥ LEGACY

The ancient Egyptians invented the first bathrooms, which were small waterproof rooms made of stone.

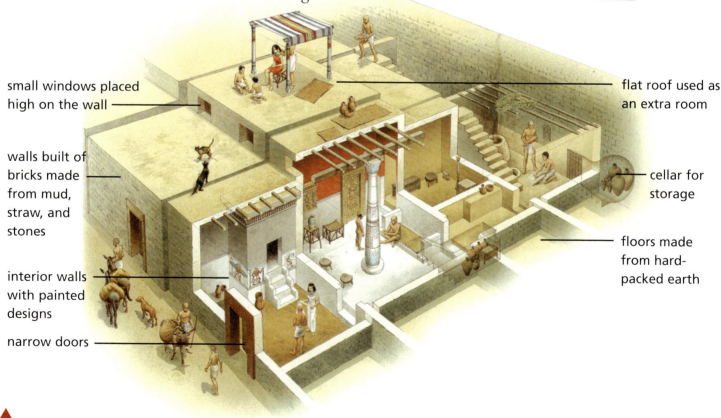

- small windows placed high on the wall
- walls built of bricks made from mud, straw, and stones
- interior walls with painted designs
- narrow doors
- flat roof used as an extra room
- cellar for storage
- floors made from hard-packed earth

Furniture

Most ancient Egyptian homes had very few furnishings. The simple furniture included stools, tables, and beds. Sometimes, Egyptians squatted on mats or cushions on the floor. Mats and curtains were made of woven reeds and decorated with coloured fabric. There were no cupboards in their homes. Storage chests made of wood or woven reeds were used instead.

Wealthy Egyptians owned beautifully carved wooden tables, chests made of imported ivory, and magnificent glass and stone jars. Their chairs had carved wooden frames and low seats made from woven cord. The short legs were often carved to resemble a lion's paws or a bull's hooves.

Lamps were stone or pottery bowls filled with oil. The wick was made of flax. Lamps were only lit for short periods of time in the evening. People went to bed as soon as it got dark and got up at sunrise to make the most of the daylight.

Pottery lamps that burned olive or palm-nut oil provided light in ancient Egyptian homes.

Beds were made of wood and woven reeds. They had wooden or stone headrests that were padded with cushions.

Some stools and tables were designed with three legs. Clothing and belongings were commonly stored in simple wooden chests or baskets of various sizes.

Stools came in a variety of styles, from simple, low structures to elaborately decorated models with carved legs. Everyone used stools, but only royalty and people of high rank used chairs.

Do 🔆 Discuss 🔆 Discover

1. With a partner, discuss how ancient Egyptian homes were influenced by the environment.
2. Use the information on pages 14, 18, and 19 to help you make notes on ancient Egyptian homes. Remember to include information provided in the text, illustrations, and captions.

Clothing

Ancient Egyptians made **linen** from flax plants. They made loose clothing from finely woven, undyed linen. It was light, cool, and suited to their daily needs. Most clothing was white, but some colourful and patterned examples have been found in tombs.

Men wore kilts that varied in length from the waist to the knee, calf, or ankle, depending on their jobs, ages, or ranks. Pharaohs and nobles wore beaded or leather belts. Women who did heavy work wore short skirts, but usually women wore longer **tunics** held in place by short straps. Because Egypt was very hot most of the year, children often wore no clothes.

People washed clothes in the river or canal. They rinsed and pounded them on stones and then bleached them in the sun. Servants washed clothes for the wealthy.

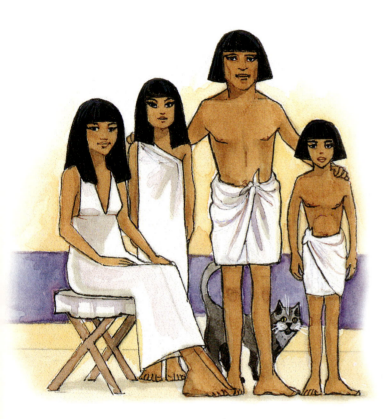

Pharaohs and nobles wore pleated linen kilts.

Cleanliness was important to the Egyptians. They washed before dressing.

Sandals were made from woven reeds. The Egyptians usually went barefoot and carried their sandals, wearing them only when needed.

Do ✋ Discuss ✋ Discover

1. In your notebook, illustrate examples of ancient Egyptian clothing. Explain how it was suitable for the climate.

2. With a partner, discuss why you think the ancient Egyptians carried their sandals.

Cosmetics

Ancient Egyptians cared about their appearance. They used cosmetics and scented oils or creams. Perfumes were made from flowers and other aromatic substances. Lipstick was made of red clay called **ochre** mixed with oil or fat. Cones of perfumed wax were sometimes worn on the head. The wax melted and flowed down to cool and give fragrance to the hair and face.

Both men and women outlined their eyes with **kohl**, a black or grey powder cosmetic.

Kohl was made by grinding the mineral galena (left) and mixing it with water. It was stored in jars and applied with sticks. The mineral malachite (right) was used to make green eye paint.

Hair

Men and women were very particular about their hair. Nobles wore wigs for special occasions. They sometimes coloured their hair with **henna**, a reddish-brown dye made from plants.

Jewellery

For special occasions, both men and women wore many pieces of jewellery made of gold, silver, copper, beads, or semi-precious stones. Nobles' jewellery often included a rare imported blue stone called lapis lazuli. Egyptians wore crowns called **diadems** that were made of precious metal and gemstones. They also wore earrings, necklaces, bracelets, rings, and wide collars made of beads.

Grooming aids such as combs, flint blades for razors, tweezers, and mirrors were used by the ancient Egyptians.

LEGACY

Nefertiti was an important queen in ancient times. She was considered very beautiful. Today, her image is often used for advertising beauty products such as perfumes or cosmetics.

Health

The ancient Egyptians had medical treatments for many illnesses. They believed that sickness came from evil spirits. When their medical treatment failed, doctors or priests would attempt to heal the person by reciting spells or recommending magic potions or prayers to the gods. Sometimes, they recommended that **amulets** be worn. They believed these charms would protect people from evil.

Doctors in ancient Egypt learned many things about the body by preparing bodies for burial and butchering animals. They knew that the pulse was associated with the heart and that fluids of blood, tears, and mucus circulated through the body.

The wedjat eye was believed to be a powerful amulet for protection and healing. It was sometimes worn on necklaces, bracelets, and rings.

Doctors kept careful records of cases they treated so they would know what worked best for particular ailments. Some doctors were specialists in areas such as women's diseases, the eyes, the stomach, or dentistry.

Broken bones were set with wooden splints bound with plant fibres. They also performed surgery with knives, forceps, and metal or wooden probes.

Many diseases were treated with plant remedies. Herbal medicines were made by mixing herbs with beer, cows' milk, or castor oil. Garlic and juniper berries were valued for their medicinal qualities. Sometimes, potions were made with disgusting ingredients in the hope that a disease or evil spirit would be driven away.

Ancient Diseases

Archaeologists have learned about illnesses and diseases of ancient Egyptians by examining preserved remains of people found in ancient tombs. Papyrus records from 1500 BCE tell us that ancient Egyptians suffered from such diseases and ailments as ear infections, tuberculosis, pneumonia, and polio.

☥ LEGACY

The Egyptians used honey, myrrh, and various spices for antiseptics. They made the first adhesive bandages by spreading honey and myrrh on strips of linen.

Using Your Learning

Knowledge and Understanding

1. Make a web in your notes like the one shown below. Complete the web to show how the ancient Egyptians met their basic needs.

2. Add the vocabulary words from Chapter 2 to your Vocabulary File. Remember to include definitions and leave room to add pictures later.

Inquiry/Research and Communication Skills

3. Use an encyclopedia or the Internet to find out more about flax and linen. For example, go to http://nefertiti.iwebland.com/index.html. Click on "Life in Ancient Egypt" and then "Linen." You could also try http://www.angelfire.com/biz7/robert20016/links.html. Click on "Origin of Flax and Linen." Record the information in your notes.

4. Prepare a flyer that might have been distributed with an ancient Egyptian newspaper. Your flyer should advertise food, clothing, furniture, cosmetics, and luxury items that could be found at the market.

Application

5. With a partner, plan an ancient Egyptian banquet. Plan the menu, how the food will be served, and what you will wear for the occasion.

6. Make a chart to compare the way that the ancient Egyptians met their basic needs with the way that the ancient Greeks and Chinese met these needs.

economic life · social life · political life · culture · the environment

Chapter 3
Work and Trade

Work and trade belong to the economic part of a culture. The ancient Egyptians worked to produce things that they needed and other things that they enjoyed. They also produced more than they needed of certain products. They could trade this surplus with other countries for products that were not available in Egypt.

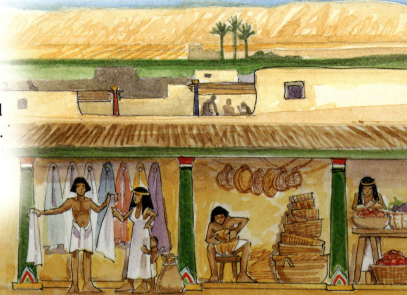

Focus on Learning

In this chapter you will learn about
- the economic life of ancient Egypt
- how their work enabled the Egyptians to meet their needs
- farming, fishing, hunting, and mining in ancient Egypt
- how artisans, craftspeople, merchants, and business people contributed to meeting basic needs
- trade between the Egyptians and people of other places

Vocabulary

nilometer	chariot
thresh	barter
chaff	

Economic Life in Ancient Egypt

The Egyptians considered farming an essential occupation. Farmers grew crops that provided food for the whole population. They also grew flax for making linen. Some farming families had just enough land to grow food for themselves. Others had enough land to produce surplus crops for trade.

Many Egyptian families made their living by fishing. The Pharaonic Village (above) near Cairo is a living history museum where visitors can see traditional fishing methods and other examples of ancient Egyptian life.

Many hands were needed during harvest. Farmers worked together to cut fields of barley and wheat.

Occupations

People doing many different kinds of jobs supported the economy of ancient Egypt. Farmers and fishers provided food. Artisans and builders created palaces, temples, homes, and items people needed for their daily lives. Scribes took responsibility for such jobs as keeping records, collecting taxes, and educating the young. Priests tended to religious beliefs and practices, and government officials managed the country.

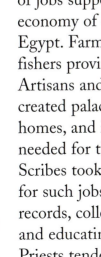

In ancient Egypt, only about two percent of people could read and write. The skills of scribes were highly valued.

Women in ancient Egypt were expected to raise the children and take care of household duties. Many also had jobs outside of the home. They worked in fields with their husbands, and some were employed in workshops or bakeries. Others were musicians or dancers in the courts or temples.

Slaves

Some slaves in ancient Egypt were people who had been captured in war. Others were Egyptians who lost their freedom because they refused to work for the pharaoh. Slaves were bought and sold in the marketplace. Skilled slaves and those trusted by people claiming to be their masters were sometimes given positions of responsibility. They might also be granted their freedom.

Do 🍄 Discuss 🍄 Discover

1. Work with a partner to list two questions that you would like to have answered in this chapter. You will come back to these questions at the end of the chapter.

Farming

Ancient Egyptian farmers divided their year into three seasons. During the inundation, from July to October, farmers could not work in their fields. They were expected to serve in the military or work for the government on a major building project.

From November to February, they prepared the land for planting by picking up stones and branches left by the flood. They marked boundaries for the fields with low mud walls or large stones. The men, women, and children of a family all helped with the farming jobs as they planted and tended their crops. From March to June, they harvested their crops.

Farmers relied on the flood water to irrigate their fields and produce healthy, plentiful crops. Farm buildings were built on higher ground so that they would not be harmed by the flood water. Egyptians used a **nilometer** to measure the flood water. Its markings or steps showed how far the river rose each year.

The amount of new farmland available for crops depended on how much soil was washed up by the flooding. After the harvest, government inspectors determined what was owed in taxes by calculating the amount of land washed up by the flood and the quantity of produce from the farmer's crop.

The Egyptians used geometry to set the boundaries of their fields after the Nile flooding.

Farm Products

Egyptian farmers grew crops of wheat and barley for making bread and beer. Fibres from flax crops were used to make linen. A variety of fruits and vegetables were grown in the warm climate and rich soil. Fig, date, and pomegranate trees were important fruit crops. Grapes were grown to make wine. Egyptians also made use of plants such as papyrus that grew along the Nile.

Farmers raised cattle, sheep, goats, and pigs that were used for meat, milk, or cheese. They also raised birds such as ducks and geese for their eggs and meat. Bees were kept for their honey. Dogs were used to tend the flocks. Donkeys helped with the work.

After harvesting the grapes, farm workers would place them in vats. They crushed the grapes with their feet to extract the juice needed to make wine.

Ancient Egyptian farmers branded their cattle with marks to show which cattle belonged to them.

Farming Technology

Egyptian farmers used various methods to assist them in preparing their land and planting and harvesting their crops.

Irrigation

Each year, the Nile River flooded between July and October. The water level fell as the flood passed down river. The ancient Egyptians needed a way to capture some of the water and save it for irrigating the crops.

They developed a system of canals, basins, and ditches built beside the fields to trap and store the water until it was needed. When the soil in the fields was dry, water was slowly released or transferred into the fields to water the crops.

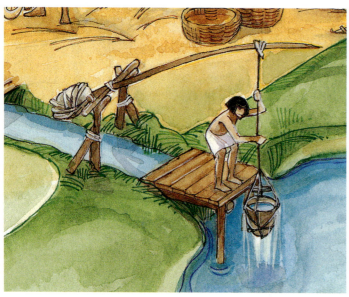

A *shaduf* was used to transfer water to the fields. The swinging beam of the *shaduf* had a heavy weight on one end and a bucket on the other. The bucket was eased into the water, filled, and lifted by means of the heavy weight.

Tools

Ancient Egyptians used hoes and ploughs drawn by oxen for turning the soft Nile soil. After the soil was prepared, someone would spread the seed by hand. The oxen would follow, trampling the seeds into the ground, and the plough would cover them with the soil.

When harvesting, the ancient Egyptians cut the grain using sickles. The grain was then spread with rakes to dry. They would **thresh** the grain by beating it with flails. Threshing separated the grain kernels from the husks, also known as **chaff**. Next, they used winnowing fans. When the mixture was tossed into the air, the lighter chaff blew away, and the heavier grain fell to the ground.

Farmers used winnowing fans to separate grain from chaff.

Farmers used hoes (middle and right) to loosen the soil for planting. Sickles (left) were used to cut the grain.

Fishing and Hunting

The Nile River was an abundant source of fish. Ancient Egyptians caught fish using harpoons, hooks and lines, or nets made from papyrus twine. Their boats were made from papyrus reeds. The reeds were tied together securely to make them watertight.

Ancient Egyptians hunted in the marshes along the Nile or in the surrounding deserts to obtain food, animal hides, or feathers. In the papyrus reeds along the river, they hunted for waterfowl using boomerangs, arrows, and slingshots. Spears were used for larger animals such as hippopotamuses or crocodiles. In the deserts, they used bows and arrows to hunt ostriches, gazelles, or hares.

Nobles hunted large game such as lions and wild cattle for sport. To pursue the animals, they sometimes used **chariots**, which were two-wheeled carts drawn by horses.

Make a Reed Boat

You will need
- a bundle of raffia, about 15 cm around and 25 cm long
- scissors
- string

1. Divide the large bundle of raffia into seven or eight smaller bundles. Trim two bundles to about 25 cm and the rest to about 20 cm.
2. Use the raffia to secure each small bundle by tying it every 3 to 4 cm along the length of the bundle.
3. Arrange the bundles side by side. Place the longer bundles at the outer sides and the shortest in the centre.
4. Place the ends of the longest bundles over the shorter ones at one end of the boat. Attach the ends of all the bundles together by winding and tying string around them. Repeat this step to attach the bundles at the other end of the boat together.
5. Secure the boat by tying it in two more places at each end, about 3 cm apart. Trim the ends of the string.
6. Finish the boat by gently forming it into a hammock shape.

Do ☥ Discuss ☥ Discover

1. a) Closely examine the illustration on this page and the tomb painting of the ancient Egyptian hunter on page 15.
   b) Make a list of everything you notice in the two images.
   c) Share your list with a partner. Discuss what you can learn about the ancient Egyptians from these images.

Mining

Egyptians loved beautiful objects, magnificent temples, and monuments. Gold, copper, and semi-precious stones such as turquoise, beryl, and amethyst were mined in the desert for making jewellery and fine objects.

This collar made of gold and semi-precious stones was discovered in a royal tomb.

This gold piece, meant to be worn on the chest, is marked with the name Pharaoh Ramses II.

Pharaoh Thutmose III presented the solid gold bowl shown above to General Djehuty to show appreciation for the general's loyal service.

In the desert, living conditions of miners were extremely harsh and dangerous. Prisoners under military command did most of the work. When it was not possible to transport mined materials by water, donkey caravans were used to carry them overland.

Gold was mined between the Nile and the Red Sea. This plentiful and highly valued metal was used for making jewellery and beautiful objects that ancient Egyptians put into their tombs. Gold was also used on statues and monuments that honoured pharaohs and gods.

Stone Quarries

Huge amounts of stone were needed to construct temples, statues, and massive tombs for Egyptian royalty. The Egyptians quarried granite and limestone from the rock formations along the Nile and the mountains near the Red Sea coast.

Some stone quarries were located near the building sites. Other types of stone had to be transported from more distant quarries. Mining and moving the stone from the quarries to the building sites required the strength of thousands of workers. Transporting the stone by boat on the Nile was easier than moving it overland.

Ancient Egyptians used chisels and hammers to quarry and shape stone. Often, stone was cut into blocks before being moved to the building site. Some stone was shaped at the site.

Artisans and Craftspeople

Skilled artisans and craftspeople were important to the economy of ancient Egypt. Craftspeople in all cities, towns, and villages made products necessary for everyday life, such as earthenware and woven fabrics. In the marketplace, people obtained all sorts of items from potters, sandal makers, basket weavers, and linen weavers.

Some artisans or craftspeople worked as teams in workshops on the estates of the wealthy, at temples, or at the pharaoh's palace. Around the temple courtyards, there were separate workshops for goldsmiths, silversmiths, glass makers, metal workers, potters, masons, carpenters, and leather workers. These workers received their wages in the form of clothing, lodging, bread, vegetables, or beer.

Whole villages of skilled artisans worked at making products for the royal palaces, such as jewellery, sculptures, paintings, and fine linens. Many of these items can be seen today in museums.

Ancient Egyptians boiled animal skins, bone, and sinew to make glue.

Lathes were used to shape furniture as early as 3000 BCE in ancient Egypt.

First Recorded Strike

Around 1156 BCE, workers building a tomb near Thebes had waited two months for their pay of food and goods. In frustration, they decided to go on strike. They sat down in the shade of the tomb calling for bread. Eventually they were paid because it was important that the tomb be finished.

These are some examples of skilled craftspeople and artisans who contributed to the economy of ancient Egypt.

The Marketplace

The towns and villages in ancient Egypt were located above the flood plain. Daily life centred on the marketplace where stalls offering many different goods filled the square and neighbouring streets.

During the New Kingdom period, Egyptians did not use money. Instead, they relied on a **barter** system. People brought items to the market and exchanged them for what they needed. A potter might trade jars or bowls for food or linen. A farmer might offer grain or vegetables as trade for furniture or sandals. The prices of most items remained the same over time. As a result, people knew what to expect in trade for their goods. Wealthy people sent their servants to shop for them.

Egypt's hot climate caused food to spoil quickly. People had to shop daily for fresh food. Ancient Egyptians could write an IOU (a promise to pay) on a piece of clay if they could not pay right away. Some people deposited grain into state warehouses. They paid for other purchases by writing orders that signed grain over to the sellers of these products.

Do 𓂀 Discuss 𓂀 Discover

1. Carefully examine the picture of the marketplace. With a partner, discuss and describe what the picture tells you about the economy of ancient Egypt.

2. Write a short story set in ancient Egypt that includes some of the information you have learned about occupations and economic life in ancient Egypt.

A Visit to the Market

Nanu and her brother Rasui were tired and dusty from working all day in the sweltering sun. Now, threshers tossed wheat into the air to separate the grains from the chaff. The children helped bag the wheat and load it into a papyrus boat. Their father, Hamul, would take it to the market in the morning and trade the grain for provisions the family would need until next harvest.

Hamul caught up to his children as they were heading home for their evening meal. "Children, I want to reward you for your work by taking you to the market with me tomorrow." The children had never been to the market in town. They cheered and jumped up and down in excitement. They had heard marvelous stories about trading ships in the harbour unloading exotic goods, and market stalls trading all sorts of fantastic things.

As their boat sailed towards town the next morning, Nanu and Rasui waved to other boats on the river. They watched an ibis fishing for its breakfast. They spotted a crocodile lurking on the shore and a catfish jumping in the water. Near town, they caught sight of a large merchant ship approaching the harbour. The children wondered about the foreign goods it might be carrying.

In town, Nanu and Rasui ran from stall to stall examining amazing items that were for sale in the market. People were busy bargaining for linens or baskets for their everyday needs. Others traded for luxury items such as beautifully decorated pottery and elegant jewellery.

Curious about the merchant ship, the children headed towards the harbour where sailors were unloading cargo. Strange-looking animals, huge wooden beams, and boxes of sparkling treasures accumulated on the dock.

Hamul, carrying two small bags, approached Nanu and Rasui. He said, "I have bargained for all of the things our family needs. I have some grain left. I want you to use this grain to purchase something for yourselves as a reward for your hard work this year." Nanu and Rasui had never bought anything for themselves. They hurried up and down the lanes of market stalls, happily searching for special items to select.

Merchants and Business People

Business in ancient Egypt involved all kinds of trade. Most merchants worked for the pharaoh. They travelled to many parts of Egypt and to other countries to barter for products that the people needed or wanted. Some goods went to the pharaoh and others were traded in the marketplaces.

At a marketplace, a fisher might trade fish for vegetables of an equal value.

In ancient Egypt, the pharaoh had final authority over all of the land. He sometimes gave land for temples and granted large estates to nobles or others who had done special favours for him. These landowners and business people became wealthy from the profits gained from farmers who rented and farmed this land.

Money and Measurement

Ancient Egyptians did not use money, so they needed a way of making fair exchanges. They used weights and measures for this purpose. Usually, a copper weight called a *deben* was used for determining the value of products. A *deben* weighed approximately 90 grams and was equivalent to 10 *kite*.

A merchant placed the product on a scale and balanced it with *deben* or other weights to arrive at a fair price for the exchange.

Products were weighed with *deben* similar to these to determine their trade value.

Volume was measured using special containers. Linear measurement (length) was based on the Royal Cubit. The cubit was determined from the length of a pharaoh's forearm from the elbow to the tip of the middle finger.

Do ☥ Discuss ☥ Discover

1. Estimate how long a cubit would be in centimetres. Explain your reasoning.

2. With a partner, discuss and list problems related to determining the value of a product using weights.

3. With a partner, prepare a skit about bartering. Present it to another pair.

Trade

Egypt became one of the wealthiest countries in the ancient world through its trade with other countries. The ancient Egyptians traded their surplus goods with countries in the area around the Mediterranean, farther up the Nile in southern Africa, and across the Red Sea.

There were few roads in settled areas of ancient Egypt because of the Nile flooding. For this reason, the Nile and the Mediterranean Sea were main avenues of transportation for Egyptian traders. Papyrus boats were commonly used for local and some long-distance trade. For more difficult and lengthy trading expeditions, stronger sea-going ships built of wood were used.

In ancient times, trading expeditions could take months or even years. The ancient Egyptians carried their boats in pieces across the Eastern Desert and assembled them on the shores of the Red Sea.

The Egyptians also sent caravans across trade routes in the desert. Travel in the deserts beyond the flood plain was difficult and dangerous. To guard these routes from thieves, the Egyptians built forts with watchtowers.

This photograph shows a model of a papyrus boat. In 1969 and 1970, a world-famous explorer named Thor Heyerdahl built life-size originals. He experimented with sailing them on long ocean voyages.

During her reign, Queen Hatshepsut sent five merchant ships on a trading expedition to Punt. The model ship shown here is based on pictures found in her temple. The actual ship was about 24 metres long.

Exports

Good farming conditions enabled the Egyptians to produce surpluses of agricultural products such as grain, papyrus, and flax. Craftspeople and artisans made linen, rope, and jewellery for trade.

The gold mined in Egypt was in demand in other countries. Egyptians traded these products for goods from other places.

Main Exports	Main Imports
gold	cedar and ebony
grain	silver
papyrus	ivory
linen	olive oil
rope	exotic animals and furs
jewellery	incense
perfume	lapis lazuli

Imports

Wood for building ships and furniture, such as cedar and ebony, was imported from other countries because Egypt had little hard wood of its own. Luxury items such as ivory, silver, lapis lazuli, and exotic animals for the palaces and temples also came from other places. Incense was a valuable import that was used during ceremonies.

At the port, customs officials made note of every item of cargo that was carried ashore. Shippers had to pay a tax on the goods they imported. Marketplaces where traders set up stalls to do business were also usually located at the seaport.

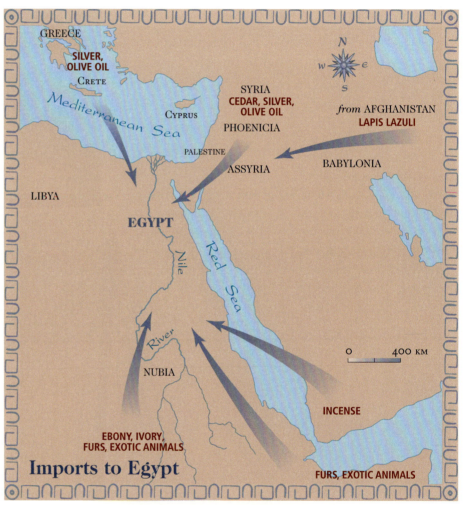

Imports to Egypt

Do ☥ Discuss ☥ Discover

1. a) Look at the trading map on this page. List the places that supplied Egypt with wood.

   b) Identify two other goods that were imported and where they came from.

   c) Share your answers with a partner and discuss why ancient Egypt became wealthy through trade.

Using Your Learning

Knowledge and Understanding

1. Parts of Egyptian economic life are listed on the chart below. Find an example of technology used for each and describe its purpose. Put your chart in your notebook.

Economic Life	Technology (Types/Uses)
Farming	
Irrigation	
Fishing and Hunting	
Mining	
Trade	
Arts/Crafts	

2. Add the vocabulary words from Chapter 3 to your Vocabulary File. Remember to include definitions and leave room to add pictures later.

3. Refer back to the two questions you developed for question 1 on page 25. In your notebook, write the answers to your questions.

Inquiry/Research and Communication Skills

4. Do research to learn about nilometers. Go to the library or visit http://www.weathernotebook.org/transcripts/1999/07/08.html or http://www.touregypt.net/feature stories/templeother.htm. Scroll to "Nilometers." In your notes, sketch an illustration of a nilometer and explain how it works.

5. Visit http://www.iwebquest.com/hotlists/egyptlife2.htm to learn about ancient Egyptian quarrying. Find out how rock quarrying today is different from ancient Egyptian times.

6. Look at the photograph and caption of the model on page 35. Visit the library or search the Internet at http://www.greatdreams.com/thor.htm or at http://folk.uio.no/janrt/hey.html. Scroll to "Ra Expeditions." Find the results of Thor Heyerdahl's experiments sailing papyrus boats across the Atlantic. In your notes, describe Heyerdahl's Ra expeditions.

Application

7. Think of words that describe what you have learned about economic life in ancient Egypt. Create a word collage on an outline map of ancient Egypt by writing words all over your map. Use colour and interesting letters. Share your collage with another student.

8. Use a graphic organizer to compare technology in ancient Egypt with technology in Canada today.

economic life | social life | political life
culture
the environment

Chapter 4
Social Structure

The roles, responsibilities, and rights of people in ancient Egypt were largely determined by the pharaoh. The pharaoh made all government decisions and had authority over all the land and monuments. Egyptians held strong beliefs about the importance of the pharaoh, and they had different roles in supporting him. They also valued family life and education.

Focus on Learning

In this chapter you will learn about
- the different groups of people living in ancient Egypt
- family life in ancient Egypt
- social activities of the Egyptians
- language and education in ancient Egypt
- Egyptian leaders

Vocabulary

descendant   cartouche
inherit   Rosetta Stone
hieroglyph   regent
script

Social Structure

Ancient Egyptian culture had several social classes. A pharaoh was the most important person in society. Ancient Egyptians believed that pharaohs were born into the family of the gods. These **descendants** of the gods were, therefore, highly respected by the people. "Pharaoh" meant "great house" and was used as we might use the terms "government" or "parliament" to refer to our leaders. With rare exceptions, pharaohs were male.

Nobles, high priests, and government officials were next in the hierarchy, followed by landowners, merchants, scribes, soldiers, teachers, craftspeople, artisans, and other professionals. The largest and lowest class consisted of farmers, fishers, labourers, and servants. Slaves were not considered part of the social structure. They had no social status or freedom unless the person who claimed to own them granted it.

Egyptians could improve their social status with education. Young boys were encouraged to learn to read and write so they could become scribes. Scribes had many advantages in society. Some wrote and read letters for townspeople, recorded harvests, or kept accounts for the army. More educated scribes advanced to positions such as priests, doctors, engineers, judges, or teachers.

Social Class

Highest Class

Pharaoh

Nobles

High Priest

Scribe

Soldier

Teacher

Craftsperson

Artist

Servant

Labourer

Farmers

Labourer

Lowest Class

Family Life

Family was important to the ancient Egyptians. Couples who did not have children would visit a doctor or pray to the gods and goddesses for help. If this did not work, they might adopt a child. Children's names were selected to show their parents' joy at their birth or to honour a special god.

Ancient Egyptians valued the wisdom of the elderly and treated them with great respect. Grandparents lived with the family. After a grandparent died, the family took food to their tomb to take care of them and nourish their spirit.

Parents' possessions were passed on to the children when the parents died. Sons were given the title to their parents' land. Daughters could **inherit** household goods such as furniture or jewellery.

Most ancient Egyptian families had pets. Cats were considered sacred. In the Egyptian religion, Bast the cat goddess, was the protector of women and children. Many cats were buried with their owners. Ancient Egyptians also kept pets such as monkeys and birds. The wealthy kept dogs for hunting.

When a pet cat died, the family would often shave their eyebrows as a sign of mourning.

Marriage

The ancient Egyptians believed that marriage was important. They married young and most often married someone from their own social class. Usually, parents chose marriage partners for their children, but sometimes couples would decide to marry without their parents' approval. Most men had only one wife. The pharaoh might have several wives.

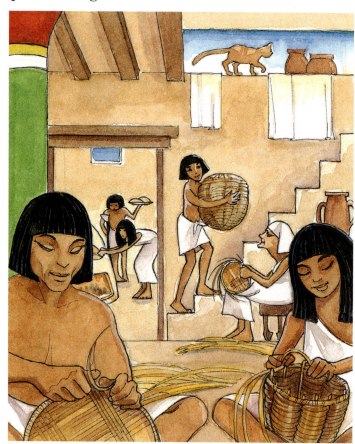

All members of a family contributed to household tasks in craftspeople's homes and on farms.

The Royal Dog

The saluki is a greyhound-like dog with feathered ears, legs, and tail. It is one of the world's oldest breeds of dog. It was the royal dog of ancient Egypt and dates back to around 5000 BCE.

Roles of Men and Women

The father was considered the head of the household and worked to support the family. A husband provided a home and agreed upon an allowance for his wife. Women raised the children.

Husbands and wives who were well off often held parties and listened to music together. Some women went hunting with their husbands. Farm wives worked with their husbands in the fields.

Women in ancient Egypt had greater freedom than women in most other ancient cultures. They could own property, but a husband usually managed a wife's land. Women in ancient Egypt also had more legal rights than women in ancient Greece or China. They could testify in court and could also bring charges against men. Some Egyptian women worked outside of the home to help support their families. They might work at jobs in business, as entertainers, or as maids. Noblewomen sometimes became priestesses.

Children

Children worked hard in the fields or workshops to help their families. They also liked to play games. They had toys such as balls, tops, and dolls. These were handmade from wood, stone, cloth, or clay.

Many ancient Egyptian games were similar to games children play today. Tug-of-war, leapfrog, wrestling, and throwing or juggling balls were popular. Swimming was also a favourite activity because the climate was so hot.

Children in ancient Egypt played with pull toys such as this wooden cat.

Do ☥ Discuss ☥ Discover

1. Look at the graphic on page 39. In your notes, explain why slaves are not included in the graphic.
2. Imagine that you are a child living in ancient Egypt. Write a diary entry describing your daily activities.

Language

The ancient Egyptian language was spoken for about 5000 years. It is no longer spoken. Egyptian people today speak the Arabic language.

Ancient Egyptians used pictures or symbols called **hieroglyphs** for writing. The ancient Egyptian written language, called hieroglyphics, contained many hundreds of hieroglyphs. Some hieroglyphs stood for sounds used in speaking, and others represented ideas or things such as a person or a town.

Ancient Egyptians recorded information about their lives on tombs and monuments. They also used brushes and paint to write on papyrus scrolls. Pharaohs and queens wore amulets engraved with their names.

Usually, hieroglyphs were written left to right, with the people and animal symbols facing right. However, sometimes they were written from right to left, with the symbols facing left, or in columns that were read from top to bottom. Scribes often used a running **script**.

This form of writing was similar to hieroglyphs, but the symbols were simplified and joined to make writing faster and more efficient.

Hieroglyphic script was carved on the sides of this monument at the temple of Luxor.

Names of ancient Egyptian pharaohs were written inside oval frames called **cartouches**. The cartouches above show the names of Pharaoh Ramses II.

LEGACY

The Egyptians developed the first calendar based on a year of 365 days.

Egyptian Numbers

Egyptian numbers were represented by hieroglyphs.

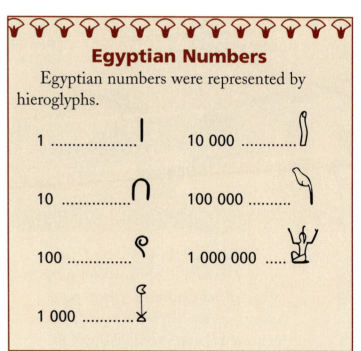

1 ....

10 ....

100 ....

1 000 ....

10 000 ....

100 000 ....

1 000 000 ....

Do ☥ Discuss ☥ Discover

1. With a partner, discuss how ancient Egyptian hieroglyphic writing and ancient Chinese character writing are similar and different.

2. Make up a math problem using ancient Egyptian numbers. Exchange with a partner and solve each other's problem.

My Own Cartouche

You will need

- self-drying modelling clay
- modelling tool (e.g., stick or pencil)
- 1 dark and 1 light-coloured paint (e.g., white, yellow, beige)
- paint brushes
- varnish
- cord (e.g., string or yarn)

1. Use the hieroglyphic alphabet shown here to practise writing your name in hieroglyphic script.

2. With self-drying modelling clay, make an oval shape like the ones shown in the samples below. Make your oval approximately 10 cm long, 5 cm wide, and 1 cm thick.

3. Use a modelling tool to make a decorative border for your cartouche.

4. Carefully carve your name in hieroglyphs from top to bottom and left to right inside the border.

5. Make a hole in the top of your cartouche and let the clay dry.

6. Paint your whole cartouche a light colour and let the paint dry.

7. Use a fine brush and dark-coloured paint to outline your hieroglyphs and decorate your border.

8. When the paint is completely dry, cover the entire cartouche with varnish and let the varnish dry.

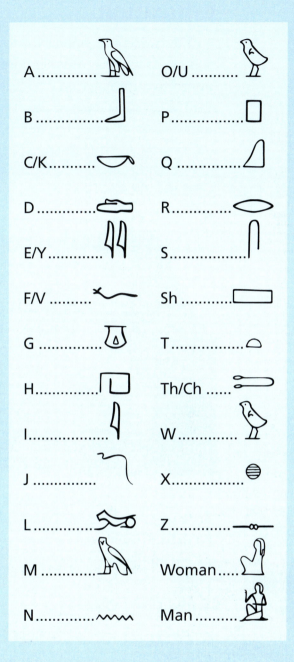

Your cartouche can be hung on a cord to wear around your neck or used as a nameplate to identify one of your belongings.

SAMPLES

Lisa   Mike

Do 𓂀 Discuss 𓂀 Discover

1. Write a short message using the hieroglyphic alphabet. Exchange your message with a partner and translate each other's message.

Education

Education was important to the ancient Egyptians. Most children did not go to a formal school to learn skills needed for their roles in life. They were taught skills at home by their mothers and fathers. Girls learned music, dance, and skills for weaving, cooking, and spinning. Boys learned farming skills or a craft.

Boys of the noble class were more likely to attend a school than other children. If they could afford to do so, families sent their sons to temples where they were taught by priests or scribes.

Students wrote on wax tablets, on pieces of pottery or stone, or with paint and brushes on papyrus scrolls.

School began at an early age. Students learned to write and read by copying and reading passages that also taught them lessons about how to behave properly. Students also learned astronomy, mathematics, astrology, arts, and sports. Boys from wealthy families were instructed in archery and horsemanship to prepare them for roles as warriors and leaders.

Boys who learned to read and write could become scribes and advance their positions in society. Becoming a scribe took many years of hard work, and discipline was very strict. There were hundreds of hieroglyphs to learn.

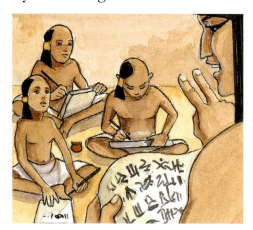

Rosetta Stone

In 1799, a stone slab was dug up near the town of Rosetta in Egypt. This stone was called the **Rosetta Stone**. It had three columns of writing. One was in ancient Greek, one was in a later Egyptian script, and one was in hieroglyphics. Scholars learned to read the hieroglyphics by comparing the pictures and symbols with the Greek translation.

Do ☥ Discuss ☥ Discover

1. In your notes, describe the education of a scribe. Include an explanation of why ancient Egyptians hoped that their sons might become scribes.

2. Use a Venn diagram to compare education in Canada with education in ancient Egypt.

Papyrus Paper

The ancient Egyptians learned how to make a type of paper from papyrus, the grassy reeds that grew in abundance along the banks of the Nile. They used the paper for keeping records and writing documents. Papyrus paper was also exported to other countries.

During the New Kingdom, ancient Egyptian artists sometimes created pictures showing animals doing human activities. This painting, done on papyrus paper, shows an antelope and a lion playing a board game.

Making Papyrus Paper

1. The papyrus reeds were cut and peeled, and the stems were sliced into strips.

2. The strips were soaked in water until they were flexible and then pounded until they were flat.

3. The strips were trimmed and placed side by side, slightly overlapping, on a sheet of cloth.

4. A second layer of papyrus strips was placed in the opposite direction across the first layer.

5. Another sheet of cloth was then placed on top and the paper was pressed to squeeze out the water.

6. A heavy weight was placed on top and the paper was left to dry.

7. When it was dry, the paper was polished with stones or wooden blocks to create a smooth surface.

Do ✧ Discuss ✧ Discover

1. a) Use a comparison chart to compare the paper made by the ancient Egyptians with the paper made by the ancient Chinese.

   b) With a partner, discuss which kind of paper you think would be better and why.

Ancient Egyptian Leaders

While ancient Greece is known for its philosophers and ancient China for its inventors, ancient Egypt is known for its great leaders. There is a great deal of information about the ideas and accomplishments of ancient Egyptian pharaohs. This exists in the form of written records and archaeological evidence. Pharaohs were considered the most important members of ancient Egyptian society.

Hatshepsut (1473 to 1458 BCE)

Hatshepsut was a **regent** or substitute pharaoh for her stepson. She wanted to rule by herself, so she convinced the priests that she was a descendant of the gods. They allowed her to become pharaoh. She increased trade with other countries and sponsored a famous expedition to lands south of Egypt.

Hatshepsut is often shown with a false beard to make her look more like a male pharaoh.

Akhenaten (1352 to 1336 BCE)

Akhenaten was a very religious pharaoh who was a philosopher and a thinker. He was married to Queen Nefertiti, who is famous for her great

beauty. Akhenaten believed that there was only one god, besides himself. He attempted to start a religion based on this belief.

This statue was made while Akhenaten was pharaoh. During this period, he encouraged artists to create more true-to-life artwork.

Akhenaten used his ring to stamp legal documents. This mark showed that he had officially approved them.

Ramses II (1279 to 1213 BCE)

Ramses II, called Ramses the Great, ruled Egypt for 66 years. He was a powerful pharaoh who was successful in many battles and gained

land for Egypt. He had a new capital city built near the Nile Delta. His magnificent monument at Abu Simbel is one of the most impressive sights in Egypt. Near it, he also had a monument built for his most beloved wife, Nefertari. He had many wives and about 150 children. He lived into his nineties.

Ramses II is shown wearing a double crown to represent his rule over both Upper Egypt and Lower Egypt.

Using Your Learning

Knowledge and Understanding

1. Select a person from one of the social classes in ancient Egypt shown on page 39. In your notes, describe how that person's work supported the pharaoh and ancient Egyptian society.

2. On a comparison chart, compare family life in ancient Egypt with family life in either ancient Greece or China. Put your chart in your notes.

3. Write each vocabulary word and its definition on a file card. On each card, use pictures similar to hieroglyphs to show what the word means. Add the cards to your Vocabulary File. Go back to the words from previous chapters and add pictures to show their meanings.

Inquiry/Research and Communication Skills

4. With a partner, visit http://atschool.eduweb.co.uk/ wheatley/Egyptian%20Web%20 Links.htm and explore some of the links about Egypt. Discuss and make notes describing how the Internet can be helpful in learning about ancient Egypt.

5. In addition to Hatshepsut and Nefertiti, Tiy was a prominent queen. Visit the website http://www.pbs.org/empires/egypt/ tiy.html to find out what made her famous and write a brief account of her importance in your notes. Include a sketch of Queen Tiy.

Application

6. Use a Venn diagram to compare the roles of women in ancient Egypt with the roles of women in ancient Greece or China.

7. In small groups, develop a skit demonstrating the lives of people in ancient Egypt. Make sure that you include the various groups in the social structure and show something about their lives. Perform your skit for another group.

8. With a partner, discuss the differences between the ancient Egyptian social structure and Canada's social structure. Write a summary sentence describing what you think is the most significant difference and why.

economic life · social life · political life · culture · the environment

Chapter 5
Religion, Arts, Sports

Religion was particularly important to ancient Egyptian society. Their beliefs about gods, goddesses, and the afterlife influenced burial customs and other religious practices. Their art and architecture show the importance of their beliefs in day-to-day life. Ancient Egyptians also enjoyed sports and recreational activities, many of which helped to prepare them for their roles in life.

Focus on Learning

In this chapter you will learn about
- ancient Egyptian beliefs
- architectural accomplishments of the ancient Egyptians
- visual, literary, and performing arts of the ancient Egyptians
- sports and recreation in ancient Egypt

Vocabulary

embalm	sledge
mummification	obelisk
sarcophagus	relief
pyramid	

48

Religion

Life for the ancient Egyptians centred on their religion. They believed their pharaoh was a god-king, descended from Amun-Re, the king of the gods. They worshipped the god Amun-Re and many other gods and goddesses.

Ancient Egyptians believed that each of their gods and goddesses protected certain parts of their lives. In their homes, they kept statues of various gods and goddesses who they believed had certain powers, such as protecting the home or ensuring a plentiful harvest.

Life in ancient Egypt depended on the flooding of the Nile. Egyptians felt they must make the gods and goddesses happy to ensure a good flood. They viewed the flooding as a sign that the gods and goddesses were taking care of them.

Holidays were celebrated in honour of the gods. *Opet* was ancient Egypt's most important festival. During *Opet*, a statue of the god Amun-Re was taken in a magnificent walk from the Temple of Karnak on one side of the city of Thebes to the Temple of Luxor located on the other side.

According to ancient Egyptian beliefs, Amun-Re was the king of the gods. He was represented as a man wearing a crown with ostrich feathers. He was also sometimes shown as a man with a ram's head.

Temples and Priests

Pharaohs built elaborate temples on large estates to honour their gods and goddesses. Each temple honoured a certain god or goddess. Priests were appointed to take care of the temples and their main duty was to look after the temple's god or goddess.

Each day, their life was dramatized. A statue of the god or goddess was taken in procession to the river and bathed. It was then returned to the temple and dressed in fine linens. Finally, food was presented to the god or goddess.

Priests lived simple lives. Cleanliness was valued, so they bathed three times a day and shaved their bodies and heads every three days. They also ate a special diet and wore white linen clothing.

⚥ LEGACY

A temple at Karnak was built for Amun-Re. Ramses II's temple is at Abu Simbel. Queen Hatshepsut had a temple (shown below) built in her honour at Deir el-Bahri. These temples are legacies of the magnificent ancient Egyptian civilization.

Gods and Goddesses

The sun god Re was the oldest and most important of the gods and goddesses. He was believed to be the father of all gods and goddesses and the creator of all life. During the New Kingdom, the god Amun was combined with Re to become Amun-Re. Ancient Egyptians considered many animals to be sacred. They used animal and human forms to represent their gods and goddesses.

Amun-Re was believed to be the lord of the universe.

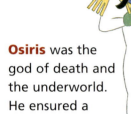

Osiris was the god of death and the underworld. He ensured a peaceful afterlife.

Isis, wife of Osiris and goddess of protection, used her power to take care of people.

Ma'at, daughter of Re, was the goddess of justice and order.

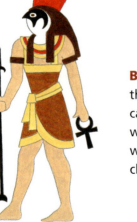

Horus, son of Osiris and Isis, was the sky god. The pharaoh was believed to be the living Horus.

Bast was the powerful cat goddess who protected women and children.

Hathor was a mother goddess in charge of music, dancing, and love.

Anubis was the jackal-headed god who guarded the dead.

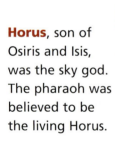

Bes was the god who protected the household and kept away evil spirits.

Do ☥ Discuss ☥ Discover

1. Use a Venn Diagram to compare ancient Egyptian gods and goddesses with those of ancient Greece.

Burial Customs

Ancient Egyptians believed that life continued after death in another form. After dying, the deceased person must appear before fourteen judges to account for their life's deeds. Anubis, the god who guarded the dead, weighed the person's heart. A light heart meant the person had led a good life. If this was the case, Horus led the deceased to Osiris to be welcomed into the afterlife.

This scene shows Anubis placing the heart of a deceased man on one side of the scale and Ma'at's feather on the other side to determine if the man lived a good life.

Ancient Egyptians believed that people needed their bodies after death, so they **embalmed** bodies of the deceased to preserve them for use in the afterlife. They used a process of embalming called **mummification**. This involved drying the body to prevent its decay.

Ancient Egyptians believed that amulets protected the dead in the afterlife. They were often placed with the body of the deceased.

Pharaohs were buried in magnificent tombs filled with riches. Wealthy, non-royal people were buried in mud brick tombs with flat roofs and sloping sides called *mastabas*. Most people were buried in public tombs. The poorest people were likely wrapped in linen and buried in shallow graves in the desert.

A wealthy person's possessions and supplies for their afterlife were placed in the tomb. This included small statues made of wood or stone. Some of these were *shabtis*, which were small figures that represented servants who would care for the deceased in the afterlife. A wooden or stone grave marker called a *stela* identified the person's name and burial place.

Mummification

It could take up to 70 days to mummify a body. All internal organs except the heart were removed. Next, the body was washed and packed in a salt-like substance to remove the moisture and dry it quickly. It was then decorated with jewellery and amulets and wrapped in many layers of linen. A mask was placed over the head and shoulders.

The mummy was placed in an inner coffin such as the one shown here. This was placed in an outer stone coffin called a **sarcophagus**. Coffins were shaped and decorated to resemble people. Those of important people were lavishly decorated.

Pyramids

Ancient Egyptians built over 90 pyramids. The pyramids at Giza required thousands of workers, millions of stone blocks, and decades to construct. These massive tombs make the nearby 20-metre statue called the Sphinx seem small by comparison.

During the Old Kingdom (see the timeline on the inside of the back cover), the Egyptians built **pyramids** as burial tombs for their pharaohs. These royal tombs are huge stone structures with four sloping triangular sides that meet at a top point.

The Step Pyramid at Saqqara, with six stepped tiers on each side, was built for the Pharaoh Djoser around 2660 BCE. It is believed to be the oldest large stone structure made by humans. The Bent Pyramid was built for the Pharaoh Snefru around 2600 BCE. Its design was changed partway through to ensure its foundation would support its weight, resulting in its unusual shape.

The most famous pyramids are at Giza. The largest, the tomb of Pharaoh Khufu, is one of the Seven Wonders of the Ancient World. The smaller two are the tombs of his son Khafre and grandson Menkaure. The Great Sphinx is a large statue that was built to guard Pharaoh Khafre's tomb. It has a lion's body and a head in the likeness of Khafre. These structures have survived for millenniums and are visited by thousands of tourists and scholars every year.

Imhotep

Imhotep is considered one of the world's first architects. He designed the first pyramids, which had stepped sides, around 2700 BCE.

The Step Pyramid contains burial chambers for Pharaoh Djoser and five of his relatives.

Architecture and Building

Ancient Egyptians constructed some of the largest structures in the ancient world. They did not have cranes, pulleys, iron or steel tools, or wheeled carts to help them. They relied on huge numbers of workers.

Ramps of stone rubble were built to raise materials. Blocks of stone were placed on wooden platforms called **sledges**. This allowed them to move the blocks forward over rows of logs. They also learned that if they made the roads wet and muddy, they could slide large objects more easily. Many Egyptian structures were so well built that they remain today.

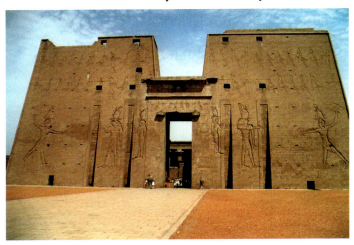

The Temple of Horus at Edfu is an example of ancient Egyptian skills in constructing mammoth structures.

Egyptian columns, like Greek columns, had many styles of capitals. Popular designs included the closed papyrus, the open papyrus, and a capital shaped like the head of the goddess Hathor.

Ancient Egyptians discovered a form of concrete. They used gypsum to bind stone and brick to make a waterproof building material.

Workers quarried huge monuments called **obelisks** from one piece of granite before moving them to a temple site. Today, obelisks (also called needles) are found in places such as Rome, London, and Paris.

Sledge Experiment

1. Try moving a heavy book across the floor by pushing it with one finger.

2. Place several pencils on the floor about 5 cm apart. Position the book on top of the pencils.

3. Try moving the book again.

4. With a partner, discuss what you discovered.

5. Decide how you would move the book across the entire room.

Do 🪽 Discuss 🪽 Discover

1. Identify each of the three Egyptian columns above. Describe how they differ from Greek columns.

Valley of the Kings

The tombs of the pharaohs were filled with valuable treasures, such as jewellery and fine furniture. Thieves often looted tombs. By the time of the New Kingdom, pharaohs were being buried in rock-cut tombs in the desert mountains to protect them from thieves. Many were buried in the Valley of the Kings on the west bank of the Nile, near the ancient city of Thebes.

The most famous tomb in the Valley of the Queens is that of Nefertari, Ramses II's queen.

Corridors leading to underground burial chambers were cut deep into limestone cliffs to protect the tombs of pharaohs from thieves. Even so, most of the tombs were robbed before the New Kingdom ended.

The Valley of the Queens is located to the southwest of the Valley of the Kings. It contains about 80 tombs and is the burial site of the royal wives of the New Kingdom and other members of the royal family.

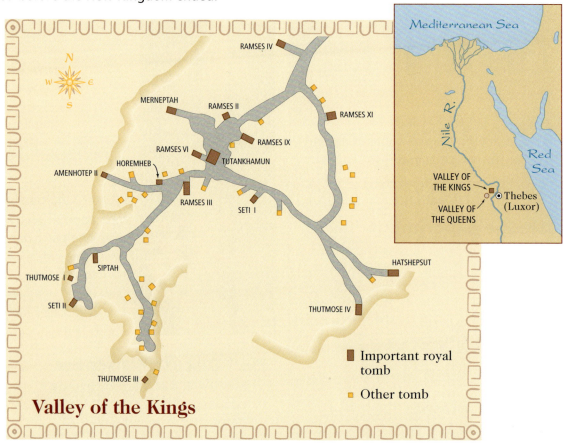

Valley of the Kings

Legend:
- Important royal tomb
- Other tomb

Tutankhamun

Tutankhamun was about nine years old when he became pharaoh and about eighteen when he died. He was not considered an important Egyptian leader, but he became famous when his tomb, filled with magnificent treasures, was discovered in 1922 by a team of researchers led by archaeologist Howard Carter.

Tutankhamun's body was removed from its sarcophagus. An examination of the body allowed scientists to learn a great deal about ancient Egyptian life. Later, his body was reburied.

Displays of the treasures from Tutankhamun's tomb have travelled to many of the world's museums, including the Art Gallery of Ontario in Toronto.

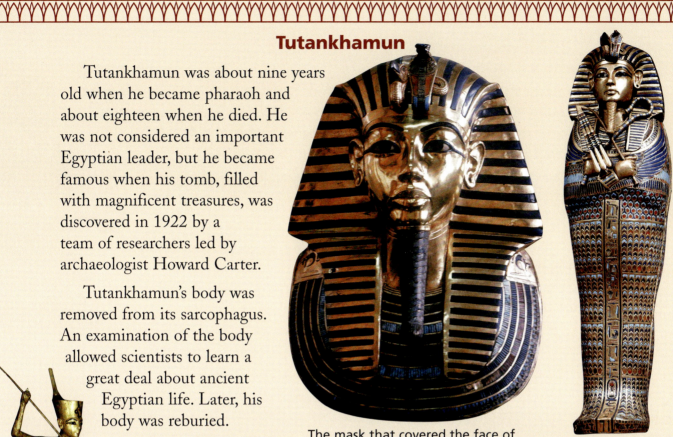

The mask that covered the face of the mummy of Tutankhamun is made of solid gold, semi-precious stones, coloured glass, and lapis lazuli.

one of the three coffins of Tutankhamun

a solid gold statue of Tutankhamun hunting

falcon amulet

scarab pendants

Tutankhamun's throne

Do ☥ Discuss ☥ Discover

1. With a group, discuss whether it was ethical for archaeologists to remove Tutankhamun's body from his sarcophagus. Use a decision-making model like the one found on page 63 in *Early Civilizations*. Defend your group's decision.

The Arts

Paintings, sculptures, and writings of the ancient Egyptians were often influenced by their religious beliefs. Clues about their values and daily life are revealed in Egyptian artwork and literature.

Visual Arts

Ancient Egyptian painters did most of their painting in tombs and temples. They covered the walls with paintings and carved pictures called **reliefs**. Many of these showed scenes from everyday life. They believed that these scenes would come to life in the next world and continue for all time.

Both arms and legs were shown, and the chest faced forward. People were represented as young and beautiful because that is how they wished to be in the afterlife.

Sculptors created all types of artwork, from gigantic statues for temples and tombs to all sorts of vases, dishes, and decorative objects. They used tools such as stone pounders and bow drills, and simple copper or bronze tools for working on stone.

Many ancient Egyptian sculptures are representations of gods or pharaohs.

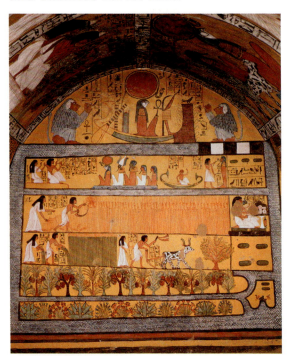

This detailed tomb painting shows a scribe and other officials supervising farming activities.

Egyptian artists followed rules in creating their work. They showed people with their faces in profile (side view) and with only one eye visible.

Glass Making

The Egyptians developed technology for making glass. While firing clay pots, they learned that the sand and slag used to make the pots melted together to make glass. They also discovered methods for colouring the glass. There is evidence that they later learned how to blow glass.

Do 𓂀 Discuss 𓂀 Discover

1. Imagine that you are an artist in ancient Egypt. Use the rules followed by ancient Egyptian artists to create a scene from your everyday life.

2. With a partner, discuss whether you think an artist should be required to follow strict rules for drawing. Explain why or why not.

Literary Arts

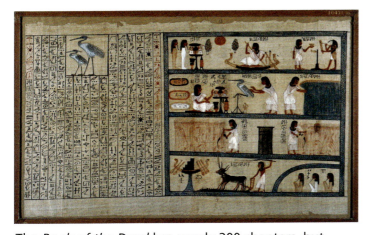

Egyptian scribes recorded details about day-to-day happenings and business on papyrus scrolls. Many of these have survived to the present. Stories, myths, and poetry provide details about ancient Egyptian activities and beliefs. Instructional texts describe their skills, such as medical practices, their study of the stars, or the mathematics that were used to build the pyramids.

A great deal of ancient Egyptian writing was religious. One of the most important works was a series of scrolls called the *Book of the Dead*. It gave instructions for the journey into the afterlife. A copy of the *Book of the Dead* was placed in the burial tomb of the deceased. Ancient Egyptians believed it would guide them in living happily in the next world.

The *Book of the Dead* has nearly 200 chapters, but copies did not contain all of them. Some wealthy Egyptians selected chapters and hired a scribe to create a special illustrated copy for their tomb. Less wealthy Egyptians would receive a standard, less elaborate version for their burial.

Myths

Mythology of ancient Egypt tells stories of their many gods and goddesses. One myth about the creation of the universe explains that at the beginning of time, there was nothing but water. A huge mound arose in the water and on it stood the sun god, Re. Re then created humans.

In one version of the creation myth, humans were made from Re's tears.

Rhodopis

This story is the earliest known version of the Cinderella story. It was recorded in the first century BCE.

Many years ago, a blonde-haired girl from Greece named Rhodopis was sold as a slave to a kindly old Egyptian gentleman to work as one of his servants.

Rhodopis's only friends were the animals. One evening, her master spotted her dancing and singing to entertain her animal friends. "How talented she is!" he thought. "I must give her some dancing slippers." The other servant girls were enraged with anger and jealousy at this gift.

One day, all of the people of the land were invited to the Pharaoh's palace at Memphis to attend a great celebration. Rhodopis wanted to go, but the other servant girls ordered her to stay behind to do washing and tend animals.

While washing clothes in the river, Rhodopis splashed her slippers. She put them on a rock to dry. Suddenly, a falcon swooped out of the sky and snatched one of the slippers. She watched as the falcon flew high into the sky. Rhodopis quickly put the other slipper inside her tunic.

Far away in Memphis, as the Pharaoh watched the festivities, the falcon flew by and dropped the slipper into his lap. The Pharaoh immediately recognized the falcon as the god Horus and knew this was a sign. He searched the land, ordering all maidens to try on the slipper so that he could find its owner.

The Pharaoh neared the estate of Rhodopis's owner. Rhodopis hid in the reeds as the other servant girls ran to meet the Pharaoh, eager to claim the slipper. The Pharaoh's keen eye spotted Rhodopis and he called her to try the slipper. It fit perfectly and she drew its mate from inside her tunic. The Pharaoh said to Rhodopis, "You are not Egyptian, but your eyes are as green as the Nile, your hair is like papyrus, and your skin is as pink as a lotus blossom. I will make you my queen."

Performing Arts

Music was popular and an important part of all ancient Egyptian religious festivals. Religious processions included musicians playing lively music on harps, lutes, lyres, tambourines, single flutes, and double flutes. Dancers in sheer flowing robes accompanied the music with graceful movements.

For special banquets, wealthy people hired musicians to accompany singers. At the same time, dancers in jewels and splendid costumes performed while guests clapped their hands or kept the beat with ivory clappers.

The ancient Egyptians did not have theatre like the Greeks. However, they did have many royal and religious ceremonies. They also had sacred dramas in which priests and priestesses acted out the lives of gods and goddesses.

Ancient Egyptians played a set of clappers by striking its two parts against each other.

Ancient Egyptian instruments and tomb paintings offer clues about what ancient Egyptian music was like.

Do ♦ Discuss ♦ Discover
1. Examine the musical instruments used by the Egyptians. In your notes, describe what you think their music was like and why.

59

Sports and Recreation

The ancient Egyptians engaged in many of the same sports and games as people today. These sports helped to prepare them for their roles in life. Games similar to hockey and a variety of ball games enabled them to develop team skills. Gymnastics, wrestling, running, and swimming were forms of physical fitness training. Sports such as rowing, javelin throwing, archery, and sports on horseback taught skills needed for battle.

Ancient Egyptians did not have public games and races as they did in Greece. Egyptians enjoyed family outings such as a day on the river and a picnic. Board games were played by adults and children. The boards and playing pieces were often beautifully designed.

A board game known as *senet* was popular with children and adults.

Do ☥ Discuss ☥ Discover

1. a) With a partner, examine and discuss the sports and games listed on this page. Which of these are similar to sports and games you play?

   b) In your notes, describe how these sports provide training for jobs that you might do in your life.

60

Using Your Learning

Knowledge and Understanding

1. Think about the religious beliefs of the ancient Egyptians. How did these beliefs influence their culture? Write your ideas in your notes.

2. Imagine you are sending news to a friend about your study of social life in ancient Egypt. Include 3 or 4 facts. Use one of the following for your message:

   • drawing (with a caption)
   • letter
   • e-mail message
   • postcard
   • story

3. Add the vocabulary from Chapter 5 to your Vocabulary File. Use pictures similar to hieroglyphs to show their meanings.

Inquiry/Research and Communication Skills

4. Use encyclopedias, resource books, or the Internet to learn more about Howard Carter, the archaeologist who discovered Tutankhamun's tomb. Use your findings to write a short biography about his life. Refer to Writing a Biography on page 123 in *Early Civilizations*.

5. Like Chinese poetry, ancient Egyptian poetry was often inspired by nature. Select one of the images in this textbook that shows the natural environment. Write and illustrate a poem expressing your feelings about it.

6. a) Go to http://www.aldokkan.com/mp3/mp3.htm to learn more about ancient Egyptian music. Click on the selections at the bottom of the website page to hear samples of modern Egyptian music.

   b) Compare ancient Egyptian instruments to those used today. How has technology influenced present-day musical instruments?

Application

7. Prepare a poster advertising an ancient Egyptian festival. Include as many of the arts as you can.

8. Read Group Discussion on page 75 in *Early Civilizations*. In a small group, imagine that you are ancient Egyptian tomb painters. Discuss the life of an important Egyptian who will be buried in this tomb. As a group, create a tomb painting representing this person's life on a large piece of mural paper.

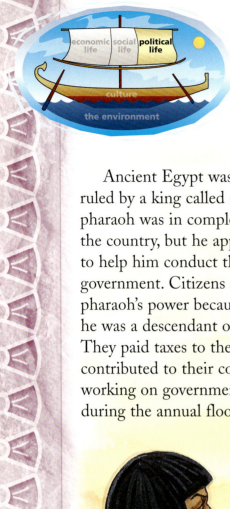

Chapter 6
Political Life

Ancient Egypt was a monarchy ruled by a king called a pharaoh. The pharaoh was in complete charge of the country, but he appointed people to help him conduct the business of government. Citizens accepted the pharaoh's power because they believed he was a descendant of the gods. They paid taxes to the pharaoh and contributed to their country by working on government projects during the annual flooding.

Focus on Learning

In this chapter you will learn about
- the Kingdom of Egypt
- the Egyptian pharaoh
- government in ancient Egypt
- Egyptian cities and towns
- the ancient Egyptian legal system
- ancient Egyptian defense and war

Vocabulary

foreign relations

treaty

famine

bureaucracy

vizier

nome

nomarch

civil servant

appeal

The Kingdom of Egypt

The kingdom of ancient Egypt lasted for over 3000 years. Egypt's history is divided into many periods, and each period is divided into many dynasties. Originally, there was one pharaoh for Upper Egypt and one for Lower Egypt. At the time of the New Kingdom, Upper and Lower Egypt were united under one pharaoh.

During the New Kingdom, Egypt was an extremely rich and powerful country. Generally, Egypt had good **foreign relations**. Its dealings with most of the neighbouring countries were positive.

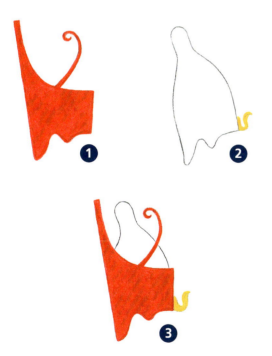

Initially, there were two crowns: one for Lower Egypt **1** and one for Upper Egypt **2**. When the regions united, the pharaoh wore both crowns at once **3**.

✢ LEGACY

A *treaty* is a signed agreement between countries. One of the earliest peace treaties ever recorded was signed by Egypt. The pharaoh Ramses II and the king of the Hittites promised to help each other when needed. The son of Ramses II honoured their treaty during a *famine*. To help with this severe food shortage, he sent grain to the Hittites.

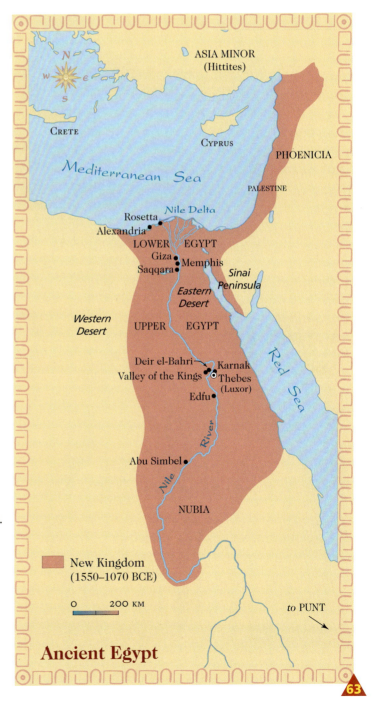

Ancient Egypt

New Kingdom (1550–1070 BCE)

0   200 KM

to PUNT

The Pharaoh

Ancient Egyptian people worshipped their pharaoh. They believed that he was a descendant of the gods and that he spoke for the gods. They thought he controlled the flooding of the Nile, the growth of crops, and Egypt's success in trade with other countries.

The pharaoh commanded the army and made decisions about Egypt's foreign relations. Rulers of smaller countries recognized the importance of the pharaoh and sent him valuable gifts called tribute to show their respect. Everything a pharaoh said or did was considered important.

Women Pharaohs

Hatshepsut was one of Egypt's female pharaohs. Another was Cleopatra, who lived much later than the New Kingdom, from 69 to 30 BCE. She was the last Egyptian pharaoh. Over the years, much has been written about her life. Shakespeare told her story in one of his plays.

The Great Royal Wife

Although a pharaoh might have many wives, he had only one queen. She was called the Great Royal Wife. It was believed that the spirit of the goddess Hathor entered the queen and she became a goddess on earth. The queen's son became the next pharaoh after his father died.

Pharaohs and queens lived in magnificent palaces, had many attendants, and took part in numerous ceremonies.

Government

Religion was a significant part of ancient Egyptian government. The pharaoh had priests to advise him, but he had absolute power. He had total decision-making power over the country's administration and courts. Citizens accepted that they had no say in government because they believed the pharaoh represented the gods.

The pharaoh appointed groups of people to help him rule. This is called a **bureaucracy**. After himself, his two chief ministers, called **viziers**, were the most powerful people. One was in charge of Upper Egypt and the other of Lower Egypt.

Official documents always carried the pharaoh's seal to prove they were genuine. This ring has Tutankhamun's seal.

Ancient Egypt was divided into 42 districts called **nomes**. Each nome had a **nomarch**, a governor who managed government business and taxation. Many scribes assisted by keeping records, collecting taxes, and doing jobs required by the pharaoh.

Structure of Government

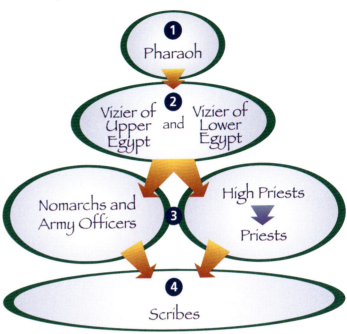

1 god-king, supreme judge, and ruler of all of Egypt

2 the pharaoh's two chief ministers

3 district and military officials, and the caretakers of the gods and their temples

4 men who kept records, collected taxes, and balanced the books

♀ LEGACY

Ancient Egyptian government workers were called **civil servants**. The title is still used today for people who work for the government.

Do 🍄 Discuss 🍄 Discover

1. What are examples of bureaucracy that you know about? Describe one example in your notes.

Hatshepsut's Expedition

Anu watched the sailors load provisions and quantities of linen, grain, and gold onto five large merchant vessels at the Red Sea port of Kosseir. After consulting with the god Amun-Re, Queen Hatshepsut ordered her advisor, Senmut, to undertake this important trading expedition to the distant land of Punt.

Anu's success as a scribe had earned him a position as Senmut's assistant. Anu had never been on a major expedition, but today he would sail with Senmut and the crew. He eagerly anticipated his adventure, but he concentrated on his responsibilities, carefully recording the goods that were being loaded. In the upcoming weeks on the voyage, he would keep detailed records of all the trading activities.

Finally, after all the sacks, crates, and baskets of goods had been loaded, the ships were ready to depart. From the deck of Senmut's vessel, Anu watched sailors in the other merchant vessels work in unison to man the large oars and move the ships out to sea. Sailors on each of the ships unfurled sails and readied them to catch the wind and propel the ships smoothly on their way.

For weeks, the five ships sailed south along the western coast of the Red Sea. Anu was delighted by the sights. High, rocky cliffs rose on the shore and unusual fish and sea creatures swam in the waters. Varieties of birds darted through the blue skies. Occasionally, Anu caught glimpses of unfamiliar animals on shore.

Eventually, the expedition reached the land of Punt. The people of Punt welcomed the Egyptians and watched curiously while the goods from Kosseir were unloaded. Once on shore, Hatshepsut's traders began to negotiate with traders from Punt. They offered Egyptian wheat and linens in exchange for precious incense and exquisite woods such as ebony and sycamore. Gold was traded for elephant tusks, monkeys, apes, and the skins of sleek black panthers. Anu worked feverishly to record the many exotic items being loaded onto the Egyptian ships.

Many weeks later, Queen Hatshepsut welcomed the successful expedition home. A magnificent procession was held to celebrate the triumph of Hatshepsut's great expedition to Punt. As the procession wound its way to the temple, Anu recalled his wondrous experiences. He was sorry to have his adventure end, but he was glad to be home to tell all his stories to his family and friends.

Cities and Towns

Egypt was mostly rural, but there were also cities and towns. These were important religious centres as well as centres for government and trade. During the New Kingdom, Thebes was the capital city of Egypt.

Great cities were built along the Nile and had harbours for shipping. Some farmers who lived outside the cities or towns used donkeys to carry their heavy loads across rough, bumpy roads to trade their farm products at the markets. Others travelled on the Nile to reach the nearest town by boat.

Each nome had a major town. The cities had wide main streets, but the side streets were narrow, dirty, and crowded.

In the cities, some people lived in poverty, but others lived very extravagantly. A number of pharaohs built splendid palaces and temples at Thebes, including the huge temples of Karnak and Luxor. Their palaces were surrounded by high walls, palm trees, and marvelous gardens.

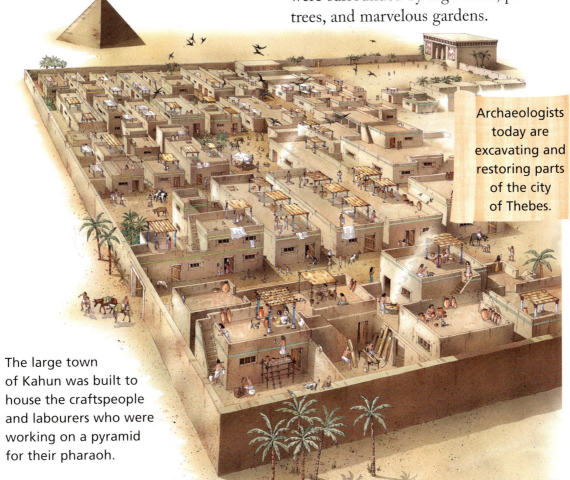

Archaeologists today are excavating and restoring parts of the city of Thebes.

The large town of Kahun was built to house the craftspeople and labourers who were working on a pyramid for their pharaoh.

Do ☥ Discuss ☥ Discover

1. With a partner, discuss whether you think it is important that archaeologists are restoring parts of the city of Thebes. Explain why or why not.

2. Examine the picture of the ancient Egyptian town of Kahun. Write a paragraph describing what you think it would be like to live in an ancient Egyptian city or town.

Legal System

The ancient Egyptians believed that people should be well behaved and that everyone should be treated fairly. They felt their legal system worked well. The pharaoh was the supreme judge and his word was law.

Ancient Egyptians often went to court to settle their differences. Men and women, rich and poor, had equal rights in the courts. Local judges handled ordinary cases in local courts.

Priests, viziers, or even the pharaoh might hear serious cases or people wishing to **appeal** a local court's decision by having their case heard again.

Depending on the crime, punishments included warnings, fines, hard labour, or even exile. Serious crimes, such as tomb robbery, received the death penalty.

Medjay

To help keep peace, the pharaoh had a type of police force called *Medjay*. These men guarded tombs, ensured the payment of taxes, protected farmers from theft, and tracked criminals. They also kept guard over the more distant and less inhabited areas of Egypt by patrolling the desert with trained dogs. Most *Medjay* maintained order in local communities. They were respected as guardians of the community.

Ancient Egyptians sometimes used baboons to sniff out criminals.

No written records of ancient Egyptian laws have ever been found. In court, there were no lawyers representing the accused. Defendants spoke on their own behalf.

Defense and War

Egypt was a powerful country with few enemies. The mountains, desert, and sea surrounding Egypt made it very difficult for other armies to attack. These natural barriers provided a type of defense for Egypt.

However, at times the Egyptians were at war. Sometimes other countries attacked them, and sometimes they invaded other countries to obtain more land or resources. For protection from invaders, the pharaoh stationed soldiers at mud brick fortresses built in the desert. The fortresses had huge walls, tall towers, and deep ditches.

During the New Kingdom, Egypt had a permanent army. Pharaohs led their armies into battle riding in wooden chariots. Other chariots usually carried two soldiers. One soldier drove the horses while the other shot arrows. Many foot soldiers followed.

Egyptian soldiers carried weapons and shields, but wore no armour. They fought barefoot.

The lion represented courage to the ancient Egyptians. In Egyptian artwork, lions are sometimes shown accompanying soldiers into battle.

Egyptian soldiers were equipped for battle with swords, spears, bows and arrows, and daggers.

Egyptian soldiers were awarded golden flies for bravery.

Do ⚚ Discuss ⚚ Discover

1. Review the information about the ancient Greek army in *Early Civilizations*. With a partner, discuss whether you think the Egyptian army or the Greek army would be most powerful and why.

2. Why do you think geographical barriers would be helpful in defending a country? Write your reasons in your notes.

Using Your Learning

Knowledge and Understanding

1. Think about the great accomplishments of the Egyptian people. In your notes, create a collage showing many of these accomplishments.

2. Use the Focus on Learning on page 62 as a guide to summarize your learning about the political life of the ancient Egyptians.

3. a) Add each vocabulary word and its definition to your Vocabulary File. Use pictures similar to hieroglyphs to show their meanings.

   b) Review the words you have learned while studying Egypt. Make up word games using some of these words. Exchange games with a partner.

Inquiry/Research and Communication Skills

4. Use an atlas or encyclopedia to find the names of countries that are Egypt's neighbours today. Label these countries on an outline map of Egypt and the surrounding area.

5. Use resource books or the Internet to find out why baboons would be useful for sniffing out criminals.

Application

6. During the New Kingdom, Egypt was a monarchy. Use a comparison chart to compare this type of government with the democratic form of government in Canada today.

7. With a small group, write a skit showing something about the political life in ancient Egypt. Perform your skit for your classmates.

8. With a partner, discuss what you have learned about the ancient civilizations of Greece, China, and Egypt. Decide in which of these you would have preferred to live and why.

CONCLUSION

Do 𓂀 Discuss 𓂀 Discover

1. Review A Model for Learning about Civilizations and the icon of an Egyptian merchant ship shown on the inside back cover of this textbook.

2. Working in a group of four, look at the illustrations shown above. Discuss and make notes explaining how each illustration represents an aspect of ancient Egyptian culture.

3. Together, assign one group member to each section of the model (Environment, Economic Life, Social Life, and Political Life). Review the chapter(s) related to your assigned section by looking at the chapter headings, illustrations, photographs, organizers, captions, diagrams, and highlighted words. Make notes describing and explaining four additional photographs or illustrations that could be added to your section of the ship to represent this aspect of ancient Egyptian culture.

4. Share your information with your group. Each group member should take notes as the others present.

5. Join one other group. Share and discuss your notes with each other. Make any necessary corrections or additions to your notes.

Pronunciation Guide

The accented syllable is underlined. All vowels are short except the following:

ay = long a (make)
y = long i (like)
oo = long u (mule)
ee = long e (equal)
oh = long o (rope)

Abu Simbel	(<u>a</u> boo <u>sim</u> bel)
Akhenaten	(<u>a</u> ken <u>a</u> ten)
Amun-Re	(<u>a</u> mon <u>ray</u>)
Anubis	(a <u>noo</u> bis)
Aten	(<u>ay</u> ten)
Bast	(bast)
Bes	(bes)
Cleopatra	(<u>klee</u> oh <u>pa</u> tra)
deben	(<u>de</u> bin)
Deir el-Bahri	(<u>dayr</u> el <u>ba</u> ree)
Djoser	(<u>joh</u> zer)
Giza	(<u>gee</u> za)
Hathor	(<u>ha</u> thor)
Hatshepsut	(hat <u>shep</u> soot)
Hittite	(<u>hit</u> tyt)
Horus	(<u>hoh</u> rus)
Imhotep	(im <u>hoh</u> tep)
Isis	(<u>y</u> sis)
kemet	(kem <u>ay</u>)
Khafre	(<u>kaf</u> ray)
khamsin	(kam <u>seen</u>)
Khufu	(<u>koo</u> foo)
Kosseir	(<u>koo</u> sar)
lapis lazuli	(<u>la</u> pis <u>la</u> zoo lee)
Ma'at	(ma <u>at</u>)
mastaba	(<u>mas</u> ta ba)
Medjay	(<u>med</u> jay)
Menkaure	(men <u>cow</u> ray)
Nefertari	(<u>nef</u> er <u>tar</u> ee)
Nefertiti	(<u>nef</u> er <u>tee</u> tee)
Opet	(<u>oh</u> pet)
Osiris	(oh <u>sy</u> ris)
Pharaoh	(<u>fayr</u> oh)
Ramses	(<u>ram</u> sees)
Rhodopis	(roh <u>dop</u> is)
sarcophagus	(sar <u>kof</u> a gus)
shabtis	(<u>shab</u> tees)
shaduf	(sha <u>doof</u>)
Snefru	(<u>snef</u> roo)
stela	(<u>ste</u> la)
Tutankhamun	(<u>too</u> tan <u>ka</u> mun)
vizier	(ve <u>zeer</u>)

Glossary

A

amulet—a small charm, worn as jewellery or placed with a mummy, believed by ancient Egyptians to protect them in life or the afterlife

appeal—a request to have a court case heard again; another presentation of a case that is heard by priests, viziers, or the pharaoh

B

barter—to exchange or trade one product or good for another

Black Land—the fertile land along the Nile River

Book of the Dead—a series of scrolls with almost 200 chapters that gave instructions for the journey into the afterlife; selected copies of some chapters would be placed in the tomb of a deceased ancient Egyptian

bureaucracy—group(s) of people who together run a government

C

cartouche—oval-shaped frames inside of which the names of ancient Egyptian pharaohs were written

chaff—husks of grain; this is separated from the grain kernels or seeds during threshing

chariot—a two-wheeled cart drawn by horses; used by ancient Egyptian nobles during hunting and by soldiers during battle

civil servant—a person who works for the government

D

deben—a copper weight used to determine the value of a product or good; it weighed about 90 grams and equaled 10 kite

delta—an area of flat land at the mouth of a river, often shaped like a triangle; several branches of the river may flow through it to the ocean

descendant—a person born into a particular family

diadem—an ancient Egyptian crown made of precious metal and gemstones

drought—long periods of dry weather with little or no precipitation

E

earthenware—pottery; ancient Egyptian dishes made of red-brown clay from the Nile River

embalm—to preserve the body of a deceased person

F

famine—a severe food shortage that puts people in danger of starvation

flax—a crop grown by ancient Egyptians; its fibres were used to make linen

flood plain—flat areas of land formed along a river when floods wash fertile soil onto the banks

foreign relations—the relationship of one country with another; can vary from cooperation to conflict

H

henna—a reddish-brown dye made from plants; used by ancient Egyptians to colour their hair

hieroglyph—a picture or symbol used by ancient Egyptians in their writing; stood for a sound, idea, or thing; together, hieroglyphs make up the hieroglyphic language

Hittites—ancient people of Asia Minor; people with whom Ramses II established a treaty

I

inherit—to receive the property or possessions of someone who has died, usually because that person has indicated that is their wish

inundation—the annual flooding of the Nile River in ancient Egypt, from July to October

K

kohl—a black or grey powder cosmetic, often used for eye makeup; made by grinding the mineral galena and mixing it with water

L

lapis lazuli—a rare blue stone that was imported to ancient Egypt

linen—fabric made from flax plants; commonly used in ancient Egypt to make light, cool clothing

Lower Egypt—the northern part of ancient Egypt; named because the Nile River flows from the higher land in the south to the lower land in the north

M

mastaba—mud brick tomb with a flat roof and sloping sides for wealthy, non-royal people in ancient Egypt

Medjay—the pharaoh's police force; they guarded tombs, ensured taxes were paid, protected farmers from theft, tracked criminals, patrolled the desert, and maintained order in local communities

monument—a structure constructed to honour or remember a person or god; obelisks, statues, temples, and tombs are types of monuments

mud brick—a building block made by mixing mud from the banks of the Nile with straw and stones, pouring the mixture into a wooden frame, and drying it in the sun

mummification—the ancient Egyptian process of embalming; preserving the body of a deceased by drying it to prevent its decay; the internal organs, except the heart, were removed, the body was washed and packed in a salt-like substance to dry it, and it was decorated and wrapped in layers of linen

N

New Kingdom—period of ancient Egyptian history from about 1550 BCE to 1070 BCE; a time when Egypt was powerful and wealthy

nilometer—steps or markings on a post used by ancient Egyptians to measure the height of the Nile River

nome—a district in ancient Egypt; there were 42 districts in total

nomarch—a governor of a nome who managed government business and taxation; each nome had a nomarch

O

oasis—a green, fertile area in the desert fed by springs of underground water

obelisk—a large monument quarried from one piece of granite before being moved to a temple

ochre—red clay, used by ancient Egyptians to colour lipstick

Opet—ancient Egypt's most important religious festival during which a statue of the god Amun-Re was carried from the Temple of Karnak to the Temple of Luxor

P

papyrus—a grassy reed that grew in abundance along the Nile River; used by ancient Egyptians for making boats and weaving

pharaoh—an ancient Egyptian monarch believed to be a descendant of the gods; the king or, in rare instances, the queen of ancient Egypt

pyramid—burial tombs for ancient Egyptian pharaohs and royal families; huge stone structures with four sloping triangular sides that meet at a top point

R

Red Land—the dry, hot, and mountainous desert land beyond the Nile River area

regent—a substitute leader; someone who governs a country on behalf of a leader who is unable to rule due to absence or illness

relief—a carved picture; often created by ancient Egyptians on the walls of tombs and temples

Rosetta Stone—the stone slab discovered in Rosetta, Egypt, in 1799; it contained three columns of writing: ancient Greek, Egyptian script, and hieroglyphics; scholars learned how to read hieroglyphics using this stone

S

sarcophagus—a coffin made of stone used by ancient Egyptians; the outer coffin that contained one or more coffins

scavenger—an animal that feeds on the dead animals it finds

script—written symbols or pictures that make up a written language

senet—a popular board game in ancient Egypt

shabtis—a small wooden or stone statue of a servant that was placed in a tomb; ancient Egyptians believed it would care for the deceased in the afterlife

shaduf—a swinging beam with a bucket on one end used to transfer water from a river or reservoir to a field

sledge—a large wooden platform on which stone blocks were moved to constructions sites; sledges were moved by sliding them (and the building materials on them) over rows of logs

stela—a wooden or stone grave marker

T

thresh—separating grain kernels or seeds from their husks by beating the grain

tomb—structure or building with a room in which a deceased person is buried

treaty—a signed agreement between countries

tunic—a loose, dress-like garment, usually reaching below the knees and having short shoulder straps; worn by ancient Egyptian women

U

Upper Egypt—the southern part of ancient Egypt; named because the Nile River flows from the higher land in the south to the lower land in the north

V

Valley of the Kings—the area on the west bank of the Nile River, near the city of Thebes, where pharaohs were buried in rock-cut tombs to protect them from thieves

vent—a small opening in the roof of the home that allowed the air to circulate, keeping the house cool

vizier—the pharaoh's chief administrator in government; there were two viziers, one in charge of Upper Egypt and the other in charge of Lower Egypt

Index

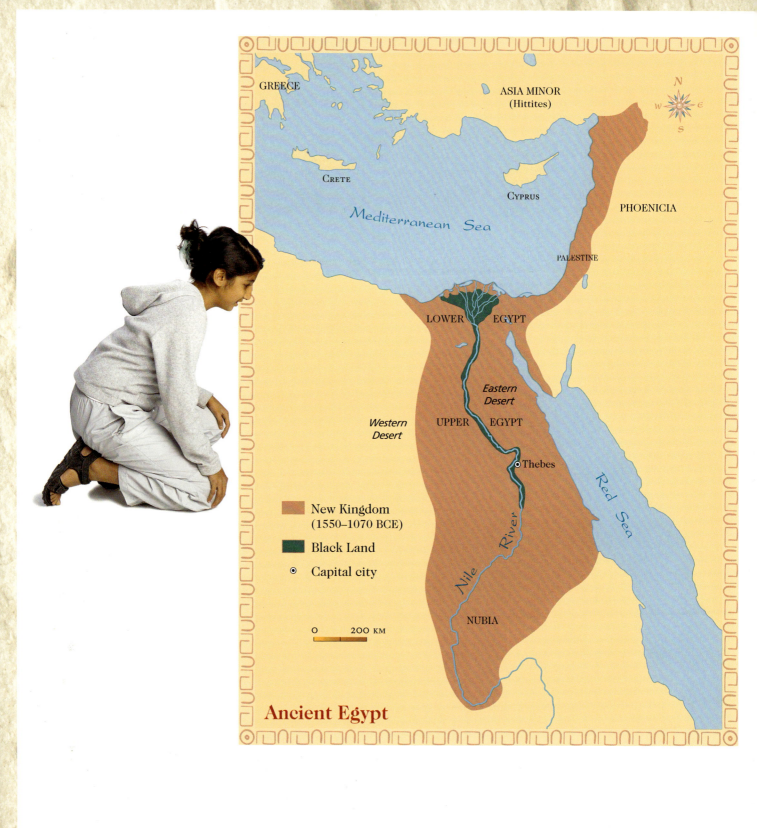

GREECE

ASIA MINOR
(Hittites)

Crete

Cyprus

PHOENICIA

Mediterranean Sea

PALESTINE

LOWER EGYPT

Eastern Desert

Western Desert

UPPER EGYPT

○ Thebes

Red Sea

Nile River

New Kingdom (1550–1070 BCE)

Black Land

⊙ Capital city

0   200 KM

NUBIA

Ancient Egypt

c. 3100 BCE
Ancient Egyptian civilization begins

c. 2686 BCE
Pyramid Age begins: First Step Pyramid built

c. 2570 BCE
Pyramid at Giza built for Pharaoh Khufu

c. 2025 BCE
Thebes becomes capital of Egypt

c. 1950 – 220 BCE
Temples at Karnak, Deir el-Bahri and Abu Simbel built

c. 1500 – 1070 BCE
Pharaohs' tombs built at Valley of the Kings

3100 3050 3000 2950 2900 2850 2800 2750 2700 2650 2600 2550 2500 2450 2400 2350 2300 2250 2200 2150 2100 2050 2000 1950 1900 1850 1800 1750 1700 1650 1600

Old Kingdom

Middle Kingdom

Scholars vary in their opinions about precise dates. Many dates are approximate.